SKILLS FOR GEOGRAPHY

PHILIP SAUVAIN

STANLEY THORNES (PUBLISHERS) LTD

Text © Philip Sauvain 1989
Original line artwork © Stanley Thornes (Publishers) Ltd 1989

All rights reserved. No part of this publication may be reproduced, stored in a retrieval system or transmitted in any form or by any means, electronic, mechanical, photocopying, recording or otherwise, without the prior written consent of the copyright holders. Applications for such permission should be addressed to the publishers: Stanley Thornes (Publishers) Ltd, Old Station Drive, Leckhampton, CHELTENHAM GL53 0DN, England.

First published in 1989 by:
Stanley Thornes (Publishers) Ltd
Old Station Drive
Leckhampton
CHELTENHAM GL53 0DN
England

British Library Cataloguing in Publication Data

Sauvain, Philip
   Skills for geography.
   1. England. Secondary schools. Curriculum subjects. Geography. Study techniques
   I. Title
   910'.7'1242

ISBN 0-85950-929-X

Typeset by Tech-Set, Gateshead, Tyne & Wear
Printed and bound by Dah Hua Co Ltd, Hong Kong

ACKNOWLEDGEMENTS

The author and publisher are grateful to the following for permission to reproduce material:

   Aerofilms, pages 57, 59, 62, 63, 105 (top)
   Barnaby's Picture Library, pages 105 (bottom), 119 (right)
   Donald I Innes, page 114
   Federal Office of Topography, Wabern, Switzerland, page 64
   Ordnance Survey, pages 47, 48, 54, 55, 56, 58
   Photosource, pages 13, 99

All other photographs by Philip Sauvain.

Every effort has been made to contact copyright holders and we apologise if any have been overlooked.

CONTENTS

PART 1: SKILLS

Geographical Fieldwork — 4

Fieldwork — 4
Ideas for topics — 5
Testing an idea — 12
Planning an enquiry — 14
Finding out from printed sources — 16
Finding out in the field — 18
Sampling — 20
Field records — 23
Measurements — 26
Field sketching and field mapping — 35
A flow diagram — 38
Maps in geographical fieldwork — 39
A land-use map — 40
Photographs and tape recordings — 42
Interviews and questionnaires — 44
Studying the evidence — 45
Skills in geography — 46

Using Maps and Photographs — 47

Mapwork — 47
Scales and measurements — 49
Directions on a map — 51
Grid references — 52
Points, patches, lines, symbols and abbreviations — 53
Maps and photographs — 60
Contour maps — 64
Drawing a cross-section — 66
Gradients and slopes — 69
Estimating area on a map — 70
Patterns on a map — 72
Map interpretation — 74

Using Statistics — 76

Statistics — 76
Graphs — 77
Averages — 81
Sampling and percentages — 82
Making comparisons — 83

PART 2: REFERENCE

Geology and Scenery — 86

Clay — 87
Chalk — 88
Carboniferous limestone — 89

Weathering and Soils — 90

Landforms on an Ordnance Survey Map — 93

The Water Cycle — 95

Rivers — 96

How a river and its valley can be used — 102

Coastlines — 104

Rias, fjords and raised beaches — 106

Glaciation — 108

Living in a glaciated valley — 109
A glaciated valley on the map — 110

Farming — 112

Industry — 114

Industrial changes — 115
Industrial sites on an Ordnance Survey map — 116

Settlements — 117

Growth of a town — 118
Town sites — 120
Functions of a town — 121
Urban hierarchies and hinterlands — 122

Pollution and Conservation — 124

Soil erosion — 126

Index — 128

PART 1: SKILLS

GEOGRAPHICAL FIELDWORK

Fieldwork

Although your home area may look unpromising and lacking in geographical interest on the surface, you will be surprised to find that if you dig deeper there are literally hundreds of different geographical topics which can be studied within a few kilometres of your school or home.

Finding a topic to study will depend mainly on what you find interesting in geography. There is little point in doing fieldwork if you are not interested enough in the subject to want to find out more. What are you most interested in? Is it people or places, or the way in which people interact with their environment? Is it the way in which people have used or abused their environment?

When you think you have found an interesting topic you will have to work out how to study it in the field. You will usually find it much easier to do this if you can think of your topic as a question to be answered – as a problem for which you will try to find an answer or, at the very least, provide information or data which could help people to understand the complexity of the problem. Best of all is a real problem which worries, excites, or interests many of the people living in your locality. For instance, you may be interested in studying what happened, or what would happen, if a local coal mine or steel works closed. Why build a new hypermarket, supermarket, or shopping centre in your town? How will it affect the community? What effect will it have on local traffic problems? Is it needed? Do local people want it? Will they use it? Where do they go now if they wish to shop at a supermarket? What effect will the new supermarket have on existing high street shops selling goods which will now be stocked by the new store?

If a supermarket really is needed, where should it be built? Which is the best location, taking into account the people who will use it and their usual mode of travel? What effect will the new supermarket have on the local environment? How will it affect local unemployment figures?

Whichever topic you choose, you will need to plan your work carefully to ensure that the fieldwork you propose to undertake is sensible and will not take up too much of your time, yet offer you plenty of scope to do some interesting work.

Urban redevelopment and the problems of the inner city could provide you with a number of rewarding topics to investigate if you live in, or close to, a large city

EXERCISES

1 Draw up a list of some of the topics which you think could be studied in your home area under some or all of the brief headings listed below:

Water	Weather
Rivers	Landscape
Farming	People
Jobs	Industries
Transport	Towns
Holidays	

2 What things interest you most in geography? Draw up a short list of some of your favourite topics. Could any of them be investigated easily within two or three kilometres of your school or home?

Ideas for topics

The topics listed in the following pages have been loosely grouped under different main headings. Some of these topics are more detailed than others and may appear to offer more scope for fieldwork investigation than other topics, which you may think too general or too thin in content. Before you begin any of these topics, you will need to consider it in relation to your home environment.

In any case, they are not intended to be treated as complete topics in themselves. Often they require similar data and information to the topics preceding them in the list. Their main purpose is to give you an indication of the range of possible topics which you could study in your home area. This, hopefully, will set you thinking. One idea often sparks off another. Do any of these topics strike a chord with you?

General geography

- A detailed assessment/criticism of a newspaper article, book, advertising or propaganda campaign, radio broadcast, or television programme which dealt with some topic of interest relevant to the geography of your home area (such as an article on inner-city redevelopment, a television programme on pollution by fertilisers, a campaign of protest aimed at stopping the building of a nuclear power station, or a broadcast discussion on the proposed closure of a railway line).

- How people of different ages, social types, jobs, and educational background, vary in the way they look at their village, town, region, or community. What do they think are its outstanding features and characteristics? What are its good and bad points? What is the town like as a shopping centre, as a social centre, as a place in which to live and work?

- The different ways in which composers, novelists, poets, artists, filmmakers and photographers have portrayed places (towns, rivers, hills, coasts, regions) in your part of Britain. For instance, you may be interested in studying the work of John Constable or Thomas Gainsborough in Suffolk, William Wordsworth in Cumbria, Thomas Hardy in Wessex, Charles Dickens in London, L S Lowry or Helen Bradley in Lancashire, Rowland Hilder in Kent, Catherine Cookson on Tyneside, Edward Elgar in the Midlands, or Dylan Thomas in South Wales.

- A survey of regional accents and local dialects. How strong and how prevalent are they in your area? Are they dying out or are they getting stronger? How do local people react to local accents and dialects? What do strangers think?

- A comparison of two communities or residential areas in your town or district showing how they differ in the quality of life they offer to the people who live there.

- The effects (or potential effects) of a major change (such as urban redevelopment, a new motorway, the opening of the Channel Tunnel) on a small area, such as a street, a village, a town, a river valley, or a farming community.

Physical environment

- Measure the flow of a river or stream at different times of the year, such as in a period of drought and after a day of heavy rain.

- Measure the flow of a stream or river at different points along its valley from source to mouth.

- Relate the flow of a river to its load (i.e. the river gravel, sand, mud, boulders on its bed which are carried along when the river is full). How and why does the load of a river or stream vary in size and type from its source to its mouth?

- Differences in the flow and load of a river or stream at different points in its course, such as (a) at a meander, (b) above and below a waterfall, (c) before and after leaving a lake or large pool, (d) near its source compared with its mouth.

Skills: Geographical Fieldwork

Contrasts often make good fieldwork topics in geography, such as a comparison between the bed of the highland stream (left) with the mud banks at the side of the estuary of a lowland river, the Great Ouse (right)

- The effects of tourism, industry, and farming on a river valley, glaciated valley, or coastline. The extent to which it has been exploited and spoiled.

- A study of all the different sources of water supply in your home area and the uses to which that water is put by industrial, business, farming, and domestic consumers.

- A study of the effects of glaciation upon a lowland area or upon a highland valley. Identification and reasoned explanation of the glacial features found there, such as drumlins, roches moutonnées, corries (cwms, cirques), erratics, tarns and lakes, etc.

- A detailed study of a stretch of beach, a cliff coastline, or a shoreline which is changing due to erosion (such as falling cliffs) or due to deposition (such as the development of a spit or offshore bar).

- A study of pollution and conservation along a stretch of coastline.

- A comparison between a coastline of erosion and a coastline of deposition.

- A reasoned explanation and assessment of the efforts which have been made to try to solve the problems of erosion and deposition at the coast (for example by building groynes and breakwaters, etc.).

- Measure the effects of longshore drift at the coast. Locate, describe and explain the evidence for longshore drift.

- A description, analysis, and explanation of the distinctive physical features on a small stretch of coast, such as a wave-cut platform, caves, arches, stacks, and beach deposits (sand, gravel, boulders, mud).

- A land-use study of the vegetation and farmland behind the high tide line – duneland, marsh, rough pasture, pine forest, etc.

- Description and analysis of the physical processes which have played their part in the shaping of a small stretch of coastline – prevailing winds, wave angles, hard and soft rocks, etc.

- Analysis and explanation of cliffs at the coastline. How and why do the cliffs vary in profile and in texture?

- An examination of the ways in which temperature, rainfall, snowfall, visibility, wind strength, etc., can vary within a relatively small area.

- The micro-climate of a small area, such as a beach, a deep-cut river valley, a park, an area of woodland, or a school playing field. Variations in temperature, rainfall, wind direction and force, and visibility, etc.

- Soil types and their characteristics. The effects of geology, climate, slope angle, etc., on soils. Variations in the nature, thickness, and utility of the soils. How they affect farming and land use in your area. How and why they change across the line of a transect, such as across a river valley or up a slope.

Land use

- How and why land use and vegetation can vary sharply within a small area, such as within the boundaries of a small town or parish or on a farm.

- How and why land use and vegetation vary along the line of a transect, such as across a river valley or up a slope.

- How land use and vegetation change the further you are from a dominating centre, such as the Central Business District (CBD) in a city centre, the pierhead in a seaside resort, or the farm buildings on a farm.

- A study of the effectiveness with which a small area, building, or project has been managed and cared for by the people responsible, such as a farm in a National Park, a country mansion, a small wood, a medieval church, or a street of Georgian houses.

- The effect of the European Community Common Agricultural Policy (CAP) on farming in your home district or in a farming district you know well.

- A comparison between two similar areas, such as a deciduous wood and a coniferous wood, a cliff coastline and a duneland coastline, a highland valley and a lowland valley. How do they differ? What do they have in common?

- Inputs, processes, and outputs on a farm. How physical factors (such as weather, rocks, slopes) and economic factors (such as market prices, government and EC policies) affect these inputs and outputs.

- Farming in a National Park. Conflicts between the needs and requirements of the farmer on the one hand and those of the conservationist on the other.

- Comparison between two similar farms, such as a dairy farm and an arable farm next door to each other, or a hill sheep farm compared with a lowland sheep farm. How do they differ? How much do they have in common?

- Examine the advantages and disadvantages, and the effects, of recent changes in farming in your area (such as the disposal of corn stubble, the introduction of new crops like oilseed rape or new breeds like Limousin cattle).

- A study of the way in which local farmers have changed, and are changing, the environment. Their attitude to the use of fertilisers, retention of hedges, stubble burning, etc.

- The changing countryside. How a rural area is changing: closure of village shops, sale of village homes to outsiders as second homes, retirement homes, or weekend cottages; closure

The work of the modern farmer often involves paperwork and work with microcomputers. If you choose to study a farming topic make sure in advance that the farmer will help you to find out about some of the aspects of farming which cannot be seen directly in the fields or in the farm buildings (such as the effect of European Community policy on farming methods)

of schools and churches; decline of rural bus services; declining employment prospects on the land; increasing pollution of the land; destruction of hedges; etc. How these changes are seen by different types of people – farmers and commuters, young and old, poor and rich, locals and newcomers to the district.

- A study of farm and land prices in your area. How and why they can vary considerably from district to district even within a relatively small area.
- An assessment of the future prospects for a local farming activity, such as dairy farming or hill sheep farming, pigs, poultry, cereals, etc.
- A detailed study of a specific farm or type of farming, such as a dairy farm, arable farm, hill sheep farm, fruit farm, market garden, pig farm, or poultry farm.

Industry

- An analysis of the inputs, processes, and outputs in some local factory, works, or industry.
- A detailed study of the relationship between a local transport system (railway, motorway, canal, port) and a specific factory, works, or industry in your home area.
- A study of a power station – its inputs (fuel and water), processes, outputs (for example electricity, waste and by-products).
- Future prospects for a local industrial activity, such as the fishing industry, a colliery, an iron and steel works, a textile mill, etc.
- A study of a specific factory or industry, such as a textile mill, an iron and steel works, a coal mine, etc.
- A study of the ways in which local industries have changed, and are changing, the environment – river and air pollution, urban development, employment and unemployment prospects, etc.
- The geographical location of industries in the local area. Reasons for the original siting of these industries. Factors affecting their later growth and development. Reasons for this continuing progress or decline, etc.
- Factors affecting industrial decisions. Recent changes in industrial methods. Their effects, advantages and disadvantages.

Transport and communications

- Prospects for the local economy with the completion of some new system of communications, such as the Channel Tunnel or a new motorway or airport.
- A study of car ownership in your district, basing your study partly on census statistics and partly on fieldwork.
- A study of the effects of restricting vehicles in specific parts of a town, such as the creation of a new pedestrian zone, imposition of new parking restrictions, or the opening of a new car park.
- A study of the extent to which people commute to or from your nearest large town. Changes in commuting patterns in the last ten or twenty years (information from the census returns). How has this affected surrounding villages?
- Declining public transport services in a rural area (for example the closure of a branch railway line). What have been the effects on the local community? How easy is it for older people to visit shopping centres, clinics, dentists, and hospitals?
- The impact of a new ring road, underpass, flyover, bypass, dual carriageway, or motorway on your area.
- Study of the traffic problem in a small town, such as the reasons why there is congestion in the town centre at rush hour. How serious a problem is it? What possible measures could be taken to alleviate the problem? What measures are actually being taken to do so?
- How does traffic flow vary along the main roads in your area? When are the rush hours? When is the volume

of traffic at its lowest? What proportion of the vehicles on the road are commercial vehicles (for example lorries, vans)? What proportion of the vehicles on the road are new vehicles? Is there any difference in the proportion of older vehicles on the road at different times of the day or on different days of the week?

- A study of the proposals being made for the re-use of a disused railway line, derelict dockland area, or former airfield. Comparison with schemes already in use in other parts of Britain, Europe, and the world.

Town and settlement studies

- What relationship is there between the position and distribution of the settlements in your area and factors such as (a) rivers and streams, (b) main roads, (c) motorways or dual carriageways, (d) railway lines, (e) airports, (f) major shopping centres, (g) major employers of labour, such as factories, ports, holiday resorts?

- Use official census data to study the population pattern of an area. Map the distribution of population. How has the population grown in the last 50 years? What changes have taken place in the proportion of local-born residents to people born in other countries or counties?

- A study of house prices in your area. How and why they can vary considerably from district to district even within a relatively small area.

- Study the influence of your nearest large town. Examine the rate at which this influence, or pull, decreases with distance from the Central Business District (CBD).

- Map the growth of a town. Study the factors which helped the town to grow in the past and how they affected the way in which the site of the town was used for building homes and industries.

- Write a case history of a new building project, such as a block of flats, supermarket, or housing estate, from planning permission to opening ceremony.

- Study the effect of building a ring road, bypass, or motorway on urban development in your area.

- Prepare an alternative view of your town or district. Contrast the rosy picture given by the official guidebook with the views and opinions of local residents.

- A comparison between two suburbs or residential districts in a town. What do they have in common? How do they differ from one another? How are they served by (a) public services (for example public transport, doctors,

Motorways speed up traffic but they also cut off people from their neighbours because access to them is strictly limited. They can even separate the fields on a farm from the farm buildings. Motorways are also noisy at night and a nuisance to people who live within earshot. If there is a motorway in your district you could study some of these effects and find out how it has changed the everyday life of local people

Market towns, like Richmond in Yorkshire, are busy enough to be interesting, yet small enough to make it possible for you to study them as a whole

clinics, hospitals, street cleaning, street lighting), and (b) private shops, post offices, banks, supermarkets, garages? How do they differ in terms of age of residents, affluence (for example proportion of cars to homes), cleanliness, age and type of buildings, etc?

- A classification of the shopping centres in your city, town, or region. Which are the shopping centres used every day for the purchase of everyday goods, such as bread, fruit and vegetables, meat, newspapers? Which are the shopping centres used for infrequent shopping, such as shoes, women's clothes, furniture, electrical goods?

- Examine the behaviour of shoppers. What shopping patterns are there in your town? What is the effect of market day on shopping? What difference is there between Saturday and Monday patterns of shopping?

- Map and analyse the hierarchy of shopping centres in your district.

- Make a detailed study of an inner-city area in need of urban renewal. Is industrial dereliction and rundown housing a problem? What possible measures could be taken to alleviate the problem? What measures are actually being taken to do so?

- City or town centre redevelopment. Evaluate the measures already taken and those approved or being planned.

- Map the variations in land use within a city. Contrast the Central Business District (CBD) with the inner city and the outer suburbs.

- Examine the extent to which shopping needs are satisfied within your nearest town, from the everyday shopping requirements fulfilled by corner shops and local supermarkets to those met by the shops in the Central Business District (CBD) and in the suburban shopping centres.

- Map the hinterland or service area of a town or city. Use data from different sources, such as school or college catchment areas, local newspaper news items and advertisements.

- Examine the extent to which the people of a village look to different towns and/or cities for employment and services.

- A study of the ways in which local planning policies affect, and have affected, the growth and development of your home area, such as their effect on an inner-city zone, on urban redevelopment, on slum clearance, on the development of new shopping centres and hypermarkets, etc.

- Make a study of the extent to which people commute to or from your home town, and the effect of commuting on the rush hour and on the development of local facilities (for example station car parks, public transport services).

Leisure and recreation

- A study of a seaside resort (or a mountain resort, such as Aviemore, Keswick, or Llanberis).
- Map and explain the distribution and location of holiday amenities and sports and recreational facilities (such as sports centres, swimming pools, fun-fairs, public houses, cafés, hotels, youth hostels) in an area of outstanding natural beauty, in a National Park, in a large seaside resort, or in your nearest town. What are the restrictions and limitations on the holiday industry (if any)?
- A study of the amenities and recreational facilities in your area. What is their effect on the town? Examine the extent to which they draw people to the town. To what extent can the town be called a holiday resort or touring centre?
- How has tourism and retirement affected your area. What have been its effects on unemployment, on the environment, on housing, on new developments, on entertainments, on shopping centres?
- How far are the recreational, leisure and sports facilities of your area (such as libraries, swimming pools, public tennis and badminton courts, cinemas, theatres) adequate for the needs of visitors or those of the people living in your district?

Pollution and conservation

- Make a survey of the litter problem in a selected area and suggest how it could be solved. How and why the litter problem varies from district to district within a large city or between villages and small towns.
- Study the effect on the environment of a particular building or feature which is regarded by some local people, rightly or wrongly, as a nuisance, such as smoking chimneys, a power station, a rubbish tip, a quarry, a prison, a football ground, a suburban shopping centre, a bypass, or a pleasure beach.
- Examine the ways in which people are affected physically by your town or village. How does your home area affect the different senses with its smells, sights, sounds, and textures?
- Pollution and conservation problems inside a National Park, in an area of outstanding natural beauty, in a holiday resort, in the countryside near your home, or in your nearest town. Conflict of attitudes between local-born people and strangers, or between farmers and tourists.
- Examine the way in which different organisations use or control natural resources in a National Park or in an area of outstanding natural beauty. How do they use its water, forests, coasts, hills, rivers, and farmland?
- Examine the effects of pollution on a stream or river. Assess the quality and purity of the water. What are its effects on the animal and plant life in the river? What are the reasons for the pollution? How serious a problem is this? What measures can (and are being) taken to alleviate the problem?

Pollution is an issue which interests and concerns most people. It offers scope for many rewarding topics in geographical fieldwork, not only at the coast and in the countryside, but also in towns and suburbs as well

Testing an idea

When you have selected a topic which you do find interesting, write down a list of questions about the topic which you think may require an answer. In particular, write down statements which can be tested in the field to see if they are true or not. For instance, suppose you want to carry out a traffic census on a local road. You might want to find out if it is true:

- that there are more Ford vehicles on the roads of your area than those of any other manufacturer;
- that there is a higher percentage of older vehicles on the roads at the weekends than on ordinary working days;
- that the period from 16.30 to 17.00 is the busiest time on the roads leading to and from your town;
- that most of the visitors at your nearest holiday resort are local people;
- that most of the heavy goods lorries on the main road are local vehicles.

An unproved statement like this is called a *hypothesis*. If you are interested in rivers, for instance, you could test out the hypothesis that the bedload of a river (mud, sand, gravel, boulders on its bed) decreases in size the further you are from the source of the river. Is it true that the flow of a river increases the nearer you are to its mouth and the further you are from its source?

You could even test the fairly obvious hypothesis that river flow is directly related to rainfall – the heavier the rainfall the greater the flow of the river. To do this you could work out an experiment to measure the flow of the river (see page 26) (a) after a period of heavy rainfall and (b) after a period of drought. In working out a method of testing a fairly obvious hypothesis like this, however, you might find that other questions or problems occur to you as well which are even more interesting than the original hypothesis:

- How quickly does rainfall increase the flow of the river?
- Is the effect noticed immediately the rain falls or is there a delay?
- If so, can the delay be forecast from the amount of rainfall which has fallen?
- Is it possible to forecast the effect that a given amount of rainfall will have on the course of the river downstream?

As you can imagine, work like this could help local people in giving them advance warning of floods.

If you would like to study the Central Business District (CBD) in your nearest large town or city you could test out the hypothesis that, on average, the buildings within the CBD are twice or three times the height of the buildings in the inner-city ring surrounding it. Or you could work out whether there is any relationship between the height of a building and its position in the town. You could test out the hypothesis that all the main transport facilities, bus stations, railway stations, car parks, are to be found on the edge of the CBD and not at its centre.

Rents are so expensive in the City of London that nowadays skyscrapers are being built so that many thousands of office workers can work (at different heights) on a plot of land which otherwise could only provide two-storeyed office accommodation for a hundred workers or so

One of Britain's leading seaside resorts – Clacton in Essex

You will find it much easier to study a topic if you can set it out like this as a hypothesis (or hypotheses if there is more than one). A hypothesis gives you something positive to test in the field. It makes it much easier and more interesting to study since you have to work like a detective, trying to find out facts which can prove or disprove a particular statement, or which can help to solve a specific problem. In this way you may be able to contribute in a small way to an understanding of the difficult problems which lie behind some local controversy, such as whether the town should have a new supermarket, hypermarket, shopping centre, ring road, or bypass.

EXERCISES

1 How could you test out the following hypotheses if you were able to carry out your fieldwork in summer at a seaside resort?
   a) That beach deposits – sand, mud, shingle, pebbles, boulders – increase in size the further you travel up a beach away from the sea.
   b) That the thickest concentration of people on a beach is always close to the main paths leading down to the beach.
   c) That the size (depth) of a beach from low-tide level to high-tide level depends entirely on its slope. The steeper the slope, the smaller the beach. The flatter the slope, the bigger the beach.

2 What possible hypotheses could you test out:
   a) On a bridge over a motorway near your home?
   b) At a railway station?
   c) At an international airport?

3 How would you try to test out these hypotheses?
   a) That towns have an influence beyond their boundaries.
   b) That the location of factories is influenced mainly by their proximity to adequate means of communication.
   c) That old industrial towns in Britain always have a Victorian inner-city ring surrounding a Central Business District at the centre.
   d) That all towns in Britain have 1930s ribbon development along the main roads leading out of town and post-war housing estates filling the gaps in between.

Planning an enquiry

Working out how to carry out your fieldwork enquiry needs careful planning, otherwise you will find that you waste a lot of time collecting unrelated scraps of information, instead of answering the main question you set out to test in the first place.

- Plan in advance the recording techniques (see pages 23–5) you intend to use in your fieldwork enquiry.

- Take care to ensure that the fieldwork can be carried out in safety. If you propose to carry out a traffic census find a safe viewpoint from which to count vehicles without danger to yourself and without getting in the way of other road users.

- Don't be too ambitious! Bear in mind that any fieldwork survey you carry out is certain to have some limitations. For instance, you will not normally be able to carry out a traffic census for 24 hours a day for a whole week. Instead you will have to sample the flow of traffic in periods of 30 to 60 minutes at a time. These sample periods may, or may not, be typical of the flow of traffic as a whole. There may also be substantial differences between summer, spring, autumn, and winter.

- Be prepared for setbacks. You may find that you are sometimes rebuffed if you try to get people to answer a questionnaire in a busy shopping centre on a Saturday. When this happens your questionnaire will only tell you about the shopping habits and feelings of the co-operative people who did have time to spare to answer your questions!

- Bear in mind, too, that some of the people you approach for information may be more anxious to tell you what they think you want to hear rather than what they really feel themselves. If it is any consolation, this also happens when researchers conduct the opinion polls you read about in newspapers or see on television.

Prepare your enquiry by following a plan like the one outlined in the chart opposite.

EXERCISES

1 **How would you plan a fieldwork enquiry to test the hypothesis that the river X is polluted by the town Y or by the factory Z?**

2 **What possible limitations can you think of to the methods you have proposed in Exercise 1?**

Fieldwork in the centre of Norwich

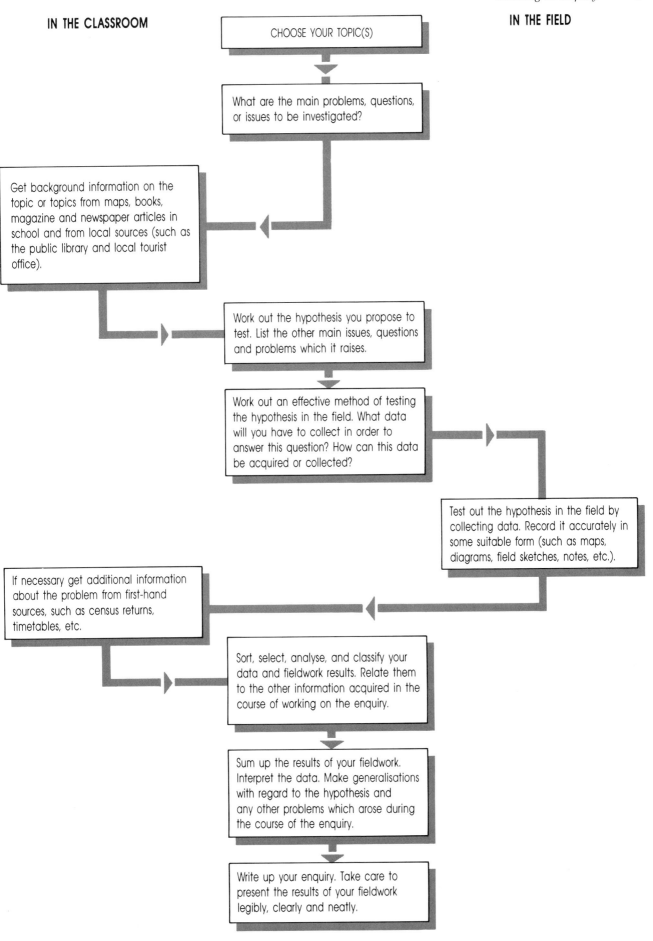

Finding out from printed sources

You can find out a lot about your topic in the library from books, magazines and newspapers; from printed statistics (such as the official census); from large-scale Ordnance Survey maps; and also from pictures and photographs (both past and present). These are just some of the ways you could use different printed sources to help you find out about a town, for example:

- *Gazetteers and year books* featuring the town, which were compiled in the nineteenth and early years of the twentieth centuries, may tell you about local businesses in the past.

- *Old newspapers* often contain advertisements for houses. From these advertisements you may be able to locate the areas in your town where new houses were being built at that time.

- *Modern local newspapers* will tell you where new housing estates are being built today in your town. You can often find out about the town's hinterland by studying other advertisements as well. How far distant do the advertisers live from the town? Plot the position of their premises on a map of the area. Link up those furthest from the town centre to show the extreme extent of the town's hinterland (or the paper's readership) when measured by local advertising. (The hinterland includes all the villages and smaller towns which are served by the town, such as the area covered by a television rental company from its head-

PINNERWOOD PARK
adjoining Pinner Hill Golf Course.
DETACHED & SEMI-DETACHED
HOUSES TO BE LET

THIS CHARMING ESTATE IS BEING DEVELOPED ENTIRELY FOR THOSE BUSINESS OR PROFESSIONAL MEN AND WOMEN WHO WISH TO RENT THEIR HOMES. Rent from £60-£83 per annum. Three or four Bed Rooms, Tiled Bath Room, Separate W.C.s, Entrance Hall, Cloak Room with Lavatory, Good Reception Rooms, Kitchen, Ample Offices Gardens laid out. Roads finished. Brick-built Garages.
The properties may be viewed on any day. Frequent Trains to City & West End. Nearest Station, Hatch End.
To view and for further particulars apply:—
Pinnerwood Park Estate Office, Dept. K, Woodhall Drive, Uxbridge Rd., Pinner, Mdx.

WEST WORTHING.
GORING HALL ESTATE.

Spacious Detached Residences,

£2,095 Freehold.

Set in the best part of this charming estate. Architect-designed and soundly built with finest materials and equipment. Containing 2 large Reception rooms, 4 Bedrooms each with lavatory basin, 2 Bathrooms, Maid's Sitting Room. Central heating. Large equipped Garage. Other types designed and built to suit individual requirements.

1.61. *Write for fully descriptive illustrated Brochure to*
NOVEAN HOMES (Worthing) LTD., 2, Sea Lane, Goring-by-Sea, Worthing.

N.W. LONDON'S NEW SHOPPING CENTRE.
COMPACT DOUBLE-PARADED.   OVER 50 SHOPS
Adjoining new Public House and Schools.
THE CENTRE OF OVER 4,000 HOUSES
(Another 500 to be erected)
SEVERAL MULTIPLES OPEN AND OPENING.
SHOPS HAVE FRONTAGES FROM 18' 0"—21' 0".
RENTS WITH 3 BED: MAISONETTE FROM £200 P.A.
Opening for most trades, and every possible assistance given to the right class of Trader.
SOLE AGENTS:—
BELL & HARCOURT LTD., 300, Neasden Lane, Neasden, N.W.10.   Gla. 5424/5.

Advertisements for housing from The Daily Telegraph, *Thursday, 13 May 1937*

quarters in the town, or the catchment area of the local technical college.) Do a similar map based on items of local news and interest in the newspaper, such as the round-up of village activities (for example the Womens' Institute) in a rural newspaper.

- *Bus, railway, and airport timetables* will help you to measure the frequency of public transport services to and from your town or city. You can easily count the number of daily services along the main routes leading into the town centre. Use a tally sheet (see page 24) to count the total number of services per day or during the course of a week. Airline services, in particular, should always be counted over a period of a week, since many flights only operate on certain days in the week.

- *Ordnance Survey maps* and large-scale plans of the district, old and new, can enable you to compare maps drawn at different times. This can help you to pick out the areas which were built over between different dates. You may be able to confirm this from your fieldwork.

- *Street plans,* old and new, can often be found in town guides and in local histories. The street names will sometimes help you to date the houses in these streets, such as King George V Avenue (i.e. between 1910 and 1936) or Balaclava Terrace (1854).

- *Local histories and guidebooks* often provide clues which can help you to work out a hypothesis which you can test in the field.

- *Old and modern photographs* of your town or district can sometimes help you to see how different parts of your town have developed in the last 100 years or so. You may be able to find pictures of the town centre before it was redeveloped or photographs which show green fields where now there are blocks of flats or office buildings.

- *Census returns,* old and recent, detail exactly the growth in population of your town and will help you to find out which parts of your town have grown more rapidly than the others.

EXERCISES

1 Where would you look for printed information which could help you to find out more about the hinterland of your local town?

2 What printed statistics might help you if you were studying the importance of a town as a route centre?

3 How do you think you could use the *Yellow Pages* in a geographical field enquiry?

4 The employment figures for Leeds in the table of statistics below were printed in the official census returns for 1961. In what ways could you use these statistics if you were studying employment in Leeds today? What do they tell you about the importance of the manufacturing industries of Leeds in 1961?

Category	Industry	Number employed
1	Agriculture, forestry, fishing	430
2	Mining, quarrying	1270
3	Food, drink, tobacco	6210
4	Chemicals, etc.	4280
5	Metal manufacture	8200
6	Engineering and electrical goods	23 000
7	Shipbuilding	10
8	Vehicles	5480
9	Other metal goods	5900
10	Textiles	6620
11	Leather, leather goods, fur	1910
12	Clothing, footwear	37 500
13	Bricks, pottery, glass, cement	2590
14	Timber, furniture, etc.	4840
15	Paper, printing, publishing	10 900
16	Other manufacturing industries	1090
17	Construction	17 150
18	Gas, electricity, water	5590
19	Transport, communications	17 160
20	Distributive trades (i.e. retail/wholesale)	45 670
21	Insurance, banking, finance	7880
22	Professional, scientific	23 660
23	Miscellaneous services	23 970
24	Public administration and defence	10 820

Total employed in Leeds in 1961 = 272 130

Source: *1961 Census Industry Tables*

Finding out in the field

The skill in finding out in the field is summed up in one simple phrase, 'Look, observe and record'. In other words, use your eyes and any appropriate measuring instruments, such as a compass, to make careful and accurate observations in the field. Ensure that you make an equally careful and accurate record of those observations.

You will find that there are many different ways of collecting and recording fieldwork information and data. Some of these methods are outlined on the following pages. But do bear in mind that no one method is suitable for all types of data and all types of situation. Choose instead the method, or methods, which you think will enable you to carry out your fieldwork quickly and efficiently.

Above all, decide *in advance* which methods you are going to use in the field rather than relying on your wits to record the things you see as you see them.

Qualitative and quantitative

Some of the observations you will make in the field will be judgements or opinions, such as a description of a valley as having 'an uneven valley floor' or annotations on a map indicating the areas of the inner city which you regard as being 'rundown' or 'derelict'. Judgements like these are called *qualitative* observations. They are usually expressed in words. By contrast, many of the other observations you will make in the field will be exact or estimated measurements, such as:

- how long, wide, deep, or high something is (for example a stretch of river 10 metres wide, 2 metres deep, 200 metres in length);

- the extent of an area (such as a 50-hectare farm);

- a measurement of temperature, rainfall, atmospheric pressure, visibility, wind direction, or wind force;

- a count, such as 600 vehicles an hour, 23 detached Victorian houses, or 39 sheep.

These are called *quantitative* observations and are usually expressed in numbers. They can be treated in special ways because they are numerical statistics (as you can see on pages 76–85).

Many of these observations, both quantitative and qualitative, can be recorded or plotted on blank maps (or *base maps*, see page 40) in the field, or on field sketches, field maps, and tables setting out measurements or comments in a clear methodical order. You can see just some of the techniques available to you if you look at the following list which shows some of the fieldwork methods which could be carried out when making a detailed farm study:

- a detailed *land-use map* of the farm (see pages 40–1), noting carefully the different crops, woodland, etc.;

- a plan of the farm buildings, indicating their main functions;

- a tracing on top of the land-use map, showing the results of some sample soil tests (see page 91) in different fields on the farm;

- a prose description of the relief of the farm, noting whether the fields are flat or gently, moderately, or steeply sloping; outlining its favourable factors, such as south-facing slopes which catch the sun; and explaining its unfavourable factors, such as heavy, badly-drained clay or north-facing slopes which are almost always in the shade;

- a map or tracing (see pages 39–41, 73) of the drainage system on the farm, showing the streams, ponds, dykes, and marshy areas on the farm, and highlighting the fields which are often waterlogged in wet weather;

- a general farm questionnaire (see page 44) asking the farmer what rotations are practised on the farm, which fields are permanently in grass, what recent changes have affected the farm, what changes have been made to the farm in recent years, etc.;

- a pie chart (see page 78) showing the relative importance of the different outputs from the farm which are sold (such as lambs, barley, milk, eggs, etc.);

- a flow diagram (see page 38) showing how the various farm inputs (such as seed, fertiliser, breeding animals, machinery, etc.) are used in different processes on the farm;

- a calendar of farming activities during the course of a typical year, together with a diary of the day's routines and how they differ in summer from those in winter;

- a table of statistics giving facts about the milk yield of the dairy herd during the course of a year.

Contrasting farms within a few kilometres of each other in Northumberland

Sampling

Making a land-use map of a farm (see page 41) is relatively straightforward, since there are only a limited number of fields to survey on the ground. Making a land-use map of a much larger area, such as the area shown on a 1:10 000 map of your district, is much more demanding. This is why we often study small samples taken at random from an area, instead of trying to cover everything in detail.

If you wanted to sample the land use in your area, for instance, you could do so by surveying two or three different farms, or by surveying a number of the 100-metre grid squares marked on the 1:1250 or 1:2500 Ordnance Survey maps (see page 47), or by studying a narrow strip of land across country. This is called a *line transect*.

A line transect

A line transect records observations and measurements made when travelling in a straight line between two points, such as a path across a river valley or a road between two villages. Observations and measurements made on a transect like this can be recorded on a *field map* like the one below (see also page 37), or on a *field sketch* showing the approximate rise and fall of the ground (see pages 35–6).

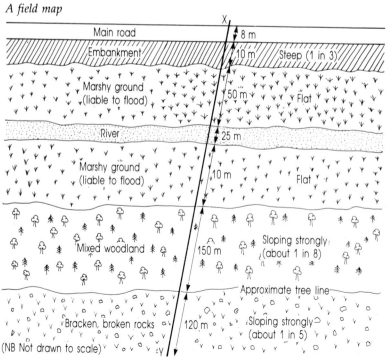

A field transect

A field map

If you survey a line transect across a river valley or up a slope like this you will, in effect, *sample* the valley or slope. This is because there is an endless number of other possible line transects which you could make across the same valley. Each of these transects, sampling land use, would be slightly different from the others. You cannot be absolutely sure that the sample you have chosen is typical of all the others.

Many of the other fieldwork investigations you may undertake in geography will be similar to this, sampling only a small part of the whole, instead of everything. For instance, you might survey only a small section of a river; study a single sample farm or factory; conduct a sample traffic count on just one of a number of different main roads; or question a small sample of the hundreds of shoppers in a supermarket.

Sampling is commonsense. After all, if you see a large box of apples in a shop you do not have to examine every apple in order to get a rough idea of their average size and weight. But beware of assuming, automatically, that the individual characteristics revealed by a simple sample must similarly apply to all other possible samples as a matter of course (see pages 82–5 on how to deal with sample statistics).

A road transect

A rough and ready land-use transect can also be made when travelling by car, bus, or train.

1. Note down the land use of each field (arable or grassland) which you pass on your side of the road or line. Note the fields in groups of ten. For example:

Fields	1st Group	2nd Group	3rd Group	4th Group	5th Group
1	G	A	G	A	G
2	G	A	A	G	A
3	A	A	A	A	A
4	G	G	A	A	
5	G	G	A	A	
6	G	A	G	A	and so on
7	A	G	A	A	
8	A	A	G	A	
9	G	A	A	G	
10	A	G	A	A	

G = Grassland   A = Arable land

2. Draw up a list showing these fields in successive groups of ten fields at a time. Work out the proportion of arable fields to grassland fields in each group of ten. In the example shown above the proportions are as follows:
   4 arable 6 grassland
   6 arable 4 grassland
   7 arable 3 grassland
   8 arable 2 grassland
   and so on . . .

3. Plot these proportions as a series of columns on a bar graph (see page 79).

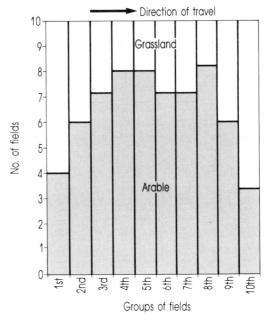

An urban transect

The same technique, using an *either/or* system of classification like this, can be used in an urban area to get a rough idea of the way in which a town has grown in the last 50 years or so. You can do this from a bus or car (if traffic conditions slow it down sufficiently).

1. Count the proportion of old or new buildings in each successive group of ten on your side of the road.

2. Classify the buildings as *either* old (over 50 years old) *or* recent (built since the end of the Second World War).

3. Plot each group of ten buildings on a bar graph or line graph.

4. Colour the proportions of old and new buildings to make them stand out.

5. What pattern can you see in your graph?

You can use the same *either/or* method to identify changes in urban land use as well:

6. Classify the buildings in each successive group of ten buildings as *either* residential *or* non-residential.

22 Skills: Geographical Fieldwork

What would an urban transect like this tell you about a town?

7 Use your graph to identify the point where the town changes from being mainly residential to mainly non-residential. Is this the outer limit of the town centre or Central Business District?

Quadrats

Another way to sample land use, apart from a line transect, is to examine in detail a very small patch of land called a *quadrat*. This is a square chosen at random, marked out by a square collapsible frame, or by posts or sticks set at the same distance apart to form a square, usually one square metre in size (i.e. four sticks one metre apart). Quadrats are useful ways of sampling soils or vegetation in a woodland area, or sampling the size of the deposits on a beach or in a river bed.

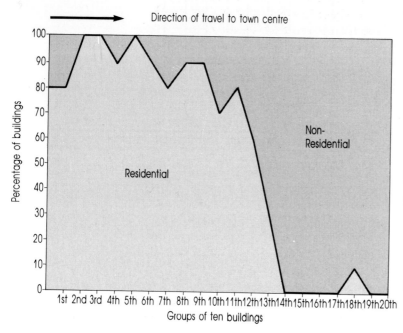

EXERCISES

1 Does the field sketch on page 20 show qualitative or quantitative observations? Which gives the better impression of the appearance of the land along the line transect, the sketch or the map?

2 What does the quadrat below tell you about the size and shape of the beach deposits sampled here?

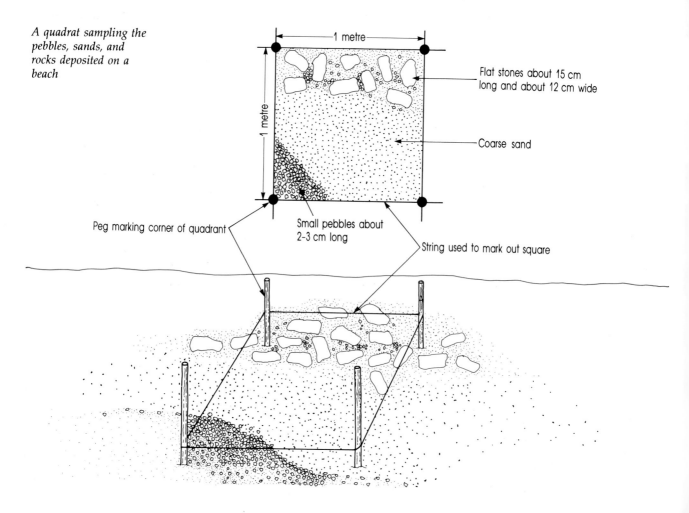

A quadrat sampling the pebbles, sands, and rocks deposited on a beach

Field records

You will need to record your observations in a systematic way, using field notebooks, questionnaires, record sheets, worksheets, or tally sheets. Many students like to take clipboards into the field, since these make it easy to keep different types of paper together, at the same time providing a firm solid base for field sketches and field maps. If you keep your clipboard inside a clear polythene bag you will even be able to make observations when it rains! It goes without saying that you should also take with you adequate pens and pencils, a short ruler, an eraser, and a pencil sharpener. You may also need to carry with you a protractor, a tape measure, a ball of string, a magnifying glass, a stop watch, and a tally counter.

When using a field notebook, or preparing record sheets in the classroom, always plan the layout of each sheet so that you can record information in a systematic way. If you need to enter information in rows and columns, rule off the pages of the field notebook or record sheet in advance. Your fieldwork observations can then be directly entered into the field notebook or on to the record sheet with the minimum of fuss.

You can see examples of different types of record sheet on this and following pages. As you can see from the buildings record card below, if details about each building are recorded in the same spaces on each card this makes it much easier to analyse and compare the different records back in the classroom. If you have access to a computer with a database program you could use record cards or sheets like these to enter details of each building into the computer. Ready-ruled record cards and sheets also help to remind you of the things you need to find out.

Buildings record cards

LOCATION	town or village
STREET/ROAD	to ensure you do not record the same building twice
NUMBER	
AGE OF BUILDING	either a year (1971) or a period (Victorian)
BUILDING MATERIALS	stone/brick/wood concrete/pebble dash etc.
NUMBER OF FLOORS	count the attic as a floor if it has a window
TYPE OF BUILDING	block of offices or flats/ detached/semi/terraced etc.
FUNCTION OF BUILDING	residential/industrial/ shop/ etc.

FUNCTION OF BUILDING	Residential

Sometimes you may only want to record whether something is there or not, such as vehicles in a traffic census. You can do this on a *tally sheet.* Mark each occurrence or presence (such as each vehicle) with a tick or a stroke. Mark every fifth occurrence by striking through the previous four, like this:

—|||| —

Tally sheets and record cards can also be used to extract information from maps or from other printed sources in the classroom, such as the *Yellow Pages.* They also help you to see at a glance the frequency with which something occurs or is present, such as the most common types of vehicle to be seen on the roads, or the most popular breed of cattle in a country area.

Fields in North Yorkshire

Area of fields	Number of fields in each size class	Total
0–1 hectares	|||| ||||		11
1–2 hectares	|||| |||| |||| |||| |||| |||| ||||		36
2–3 hectares	|||| |||| |||| |||| |||| |||| |||| |||| |||| |||| ||||		56
3–4 hectares	|||| |||| |||| |||| |||| ||	27
4–5 hectares	|||| |||| |||| |||	18
5–6 hectares	||||		6

A tally sheet used to analyse the size of the fields in a rural area

EXERCISES

1 **What does the tally sheet above tell you about the average size of field in the area surveyed?**

2 **What hypotheses could be tested on the beach using the measurements recorded in the record sheet below?**

Location	Deposits	Diameters (pebbles)	Slope of beach
Pier	fine gravel	5 mm	1°
50 m west of pier	fine gravel	4 mm	1°–2°
100 m west of pier	coarse gravel	35 mm	4°
150 m west of pier	cobbles	120 mm	4°

Analysis of the beach deposits along a coastline

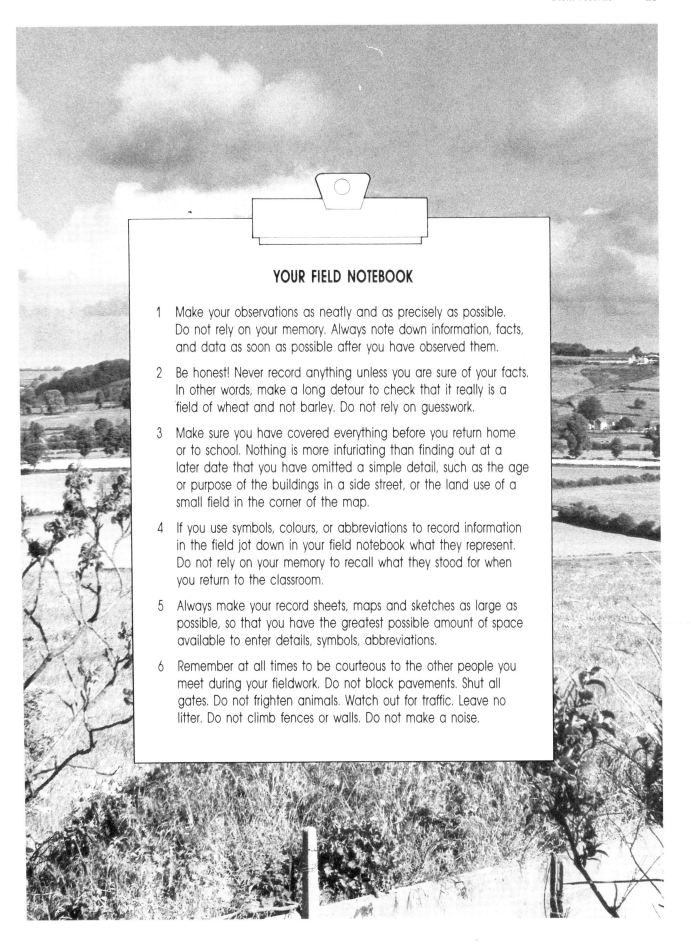

YOUR FIELD NOTEBOOK

1. Make your observations as neatly and as precisely as possible. Do not rely on your memory. Always note down information, facts, and data as soon as possible after you have observed them.

2. Be honest! Never record anything unless you are sure of your facts. In other words, make a long detour to check that it really is a field of wheat and not barley. Do not rely on guesswork.

3. Make sure you have covered everything before you return home or to school. Nothing is more infuriating than finding out at a later date that you have omitted a simple detail, such as the age or purpose of the buildings in a side street, or the land use of a small field in the corner of the map.

4. If you use symbols, colours, or abbreviations to record information in the field jot down in your field notebook what they represent. Do not rely on your memory to recall what they stood for when you return to the classroom.

5. Always make your record sheets, maps and sketches as large as possible, so that you have the greatest possible amount of space available to enter details, symbols, abbreviations.

6. Remember at all times to be courteous to the other people you meet during your fieldwork. Do not block pavements. Shut all gates. Do not frighten animals. Watch out for traffic. Leave no litter. Do not climb fences or walls. Do not make a noise.

Measurements

There are a number of different ways to take measurements of the things you see and study in the field. Which you use will depend entirely on your topic and the type of hypothesis you are testing and also on whether you have the time, the right apparatus, or the assistance of a friend. In these examples you can see only a few of the many different methods you could use in your geographical fieldwork.

Measuring the flow of a river

1. Measure first the width of the river from bank to bank at a bridge or at some other safe crossing point. (Let us take the example of a river 15.2 metres wide.)

2. Measure carefully the depth of the stream at equal intervals across its width, so that you get ten or more readings. You can do this either by prodding the river bed with a long pole or by using a piece of string with a heavy weight on the end.

3. Note carefully the wetted length of pole or string each time you sample the depth of the river. Record these depths on a chart, like the one below.

Metres across	Depth in centimetres
1	10
2	27
3	40
4	52
5	60
6	48
7	33
8	35
9	28
10	23
11	20
12	18
13	16
14	15
15	10
Total	435

4. Calculate the average depth of the river by adding up the depths in centimetres and dividing by the number of readings. (In the example the total of 435 centimetres has been divided by 15 to give an average depth of 29 centimetres or 0.29 metres.)

5. From this average depth in *metres*, estimate the area of cross-section of the stream in *square metres* by multiplying it by the width of the stream at the point where the depth readings were taken. (In the example this is 0.29 metres × 15.2 metres = 4.41 square metres.)

6. Measure the speed of flow of the river by timing how long (in seconds) it takes a feather or twig to travel a distance of 10 or 20 metres downstream. Repeat these timings at different points across the width of the river and average them out to produce an average time for the distance you have chosen. (In the example below the average time taken to cover 10 metres is 200 ÷ 8 = 25 seconds.)

Time taken to cover 10 metres (in seconds)
24 27 24 23 26 27 24 25
Total of 8 timings
200 seconds

7. Divide the distance (in metres) by the average time (in seconds) to work out the average speed of the river in metres per second. (In the example the average speed of the stream is 10 metres divided by 25 seconds = 10 ÷ 25 = 0.4 metres per second.)

8. From these figures work out the speed of flow of the river in *cubic metres* per second by multiplying the area of cross-section in square metres by the speed of flow in metres per second. (Thus 4.41 square metres × 0.4 metres per second = 1.764 cubic metres per second.)

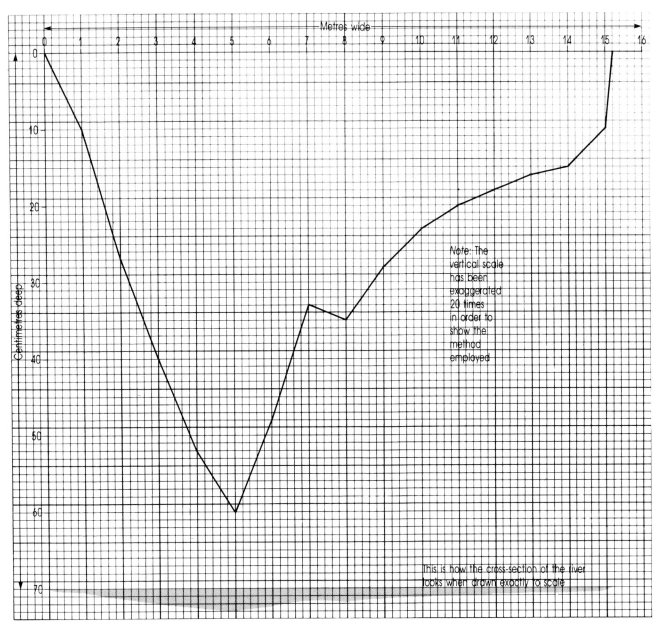

9 Since this is an estimated cubic flow, round it off to the nearest tenth of a cubic metre. (1.764 = 1.8 cubic metres per second.)

10 Once you have worked out the area of cross-section of river at a particular point across the river it is easy to work out the effect that variations in the flow of the river will have after heavy rain or drought. The river level will rise or fall by the same amount across the entire width of the river. If it rises by 0.2 metres, add 0.2 metres to the average depth. If it falls by 0.1 metres then deduct 0.1 metres from the average depth, and so on.

EXERCISES

1 **What would be the cubic flow of the river in the example on these pages if its average speed of flow was 0.65 metres per second?**

2 **Work out the cubic flow of the river if the river level rises by 0.2 metres after heavy rain and the speed of flow increases to 0.9 metres per second? The river width remains the same at 15.2 metres.**

3 **What is the cubic flow of the river if the river level falls by 0.1 metres after a drought, its width decreases to 13.4 metres, and the speed of flow drops to 0.7 metres per second?**

You can plot these depths on a graph if you want to see what the cross-section of the stream looks like when drawn to scale or when the depths are exaggerated (as they are in this graph). Use the counting squares method (see pages 70–1) to calculate the area of cross-section accurately. Divide the total number of small squares by 500 to give the area in square metres

Measuring the size and shape of beach or river deposits

For a survey of this type, such as measuring the size and shape of beach deposits at low tide or the stones and boulders on a river bed (during a drought), all you need is a tape measure and a pencil and pad to record your measurements. A series of sample measurements should soon help you to work out the average size and shape of the different deposits you encounter. Classify these different types of deposit using the table of sizes opposite.

Type	Diameter
Boulders	Over 200 mm
Cobbles	60–200 mm
Coarse gravel	20–60 mm
Medium gravel	6–20 mm
Fine gravel	2–6 mm
Coarse sand	0.6–2 mm
Medium sand	0.2–0.6 mm
Fine sand	0.06–0.2 mm
Silts and clays	Under 0.06 mm

Measuring the features of erosion and deposition

Measurement of the effects of coastal erosion and deposition at a cliff coastline (see pages 104–5), for example, can be undertaken by measuring the height, length, and width of the different features you can identify, such as caves, arches, stacks, cliffs, headlands, rock pools, the wave-cut platform, and the notches at the foot of cliffs which have been eroded by wave action. You can also measure the height of the sand or pebbles piled up on either side of the groynes. Similar measurements can be made of the characteristic features due to river action (see pages 96–100), and ice action (see pages 108-11).

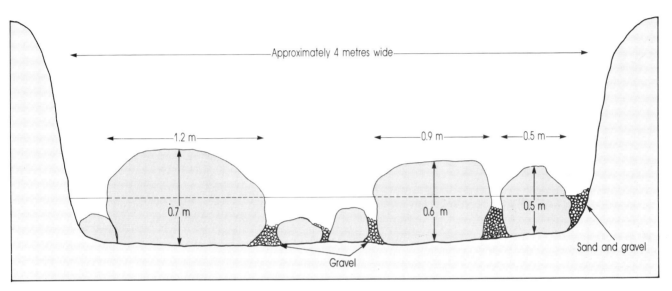

Stones and boulders on a river bed

Measure the features you can identify, either by pacing or with a tape measure. If this is not possible, then estimate the dimensions carefully. Find the height, width and depth (where applicable) of the caves, stacks, arches, cliffs and other features you observe.

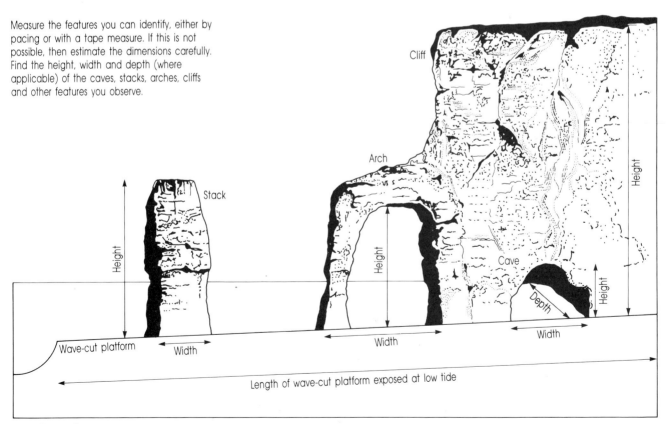

A cliff coastline

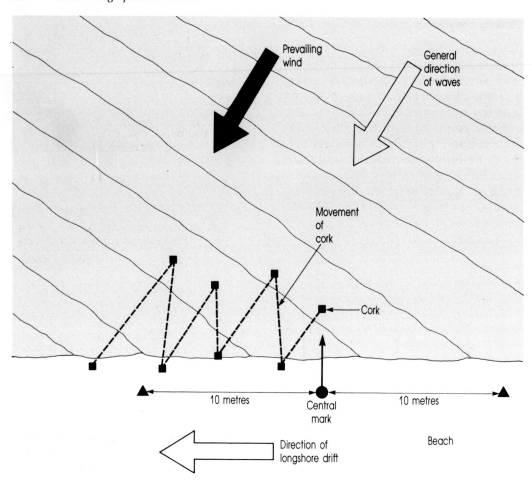

Measuring longshore drift

1. Make a fixed central mark on the beach in front of the advancing tide.

2. Measure off and mark a distance of 10 metres from this central mark in both directions at right angles to the beach and parallel with the sea.

3. Throw a cork, or some other easily identifiable object that will float, into the sea exactly opposite the central mark.

4. Count the time it takes in seconds before the advancing and retreating waves move the cork laterally so that it is thrown up on the beach past either of the two 10-metre markers.

5. Repeat the experiment a number of times until you are satisfied that the cork is being moved consistently along the beach in one direction only.

6. How strong is the longshore drift on this beach?

7. Examine the groynes on the beach, if there are any. Measure the height of the sand or shingle on either side of each groyne. Do these measurements confirm or refute your longshore drift experiments?

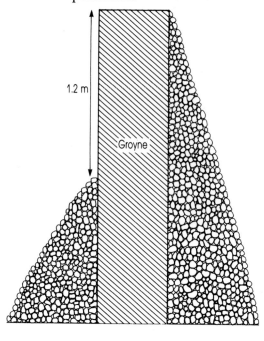

Cross-section of a groyne looking towards the sea. The prevailing wind is from the south-west

A tally counter

Many different types of survey can be undertaken by counting the frequency with which something occurs or can be observed within a specific area, along a line transect, along a road, or during a specific period of time. Studies of this type include counting the number of fields of livestock compared with those containing crops when travelling by train or bus; counting the different species of tree to be found in a woodland area; counting vehicles on a main road in a traffic census.

You will find it much easier to count things quickly, or to count large numbers, if you use a tally counter. This is a simple device which works like a mileometer on a car. Each time you click the button it moves the counter on by *one*. If traffic is very busy a tally counter is often the only reliable way to ensure that your count is accurate.

A clinometer

You can make a simple device to measure the angle of a slope of a beach, the side of a valley, or a hill, if you fix a protractor to a flat board, with a thread pendulum suspended from the central point of the protractor (like the one shown in the diagram below).

1. Place the edge of the clinometer along the slope so that the pendulum can swing freely.
2. Read off the angle made by the pendulum thread and the 90° marker on the protractor. This angle is the same as the angle the slope makes with the horizontal. (You can prove this for yourself if you study geometry.)

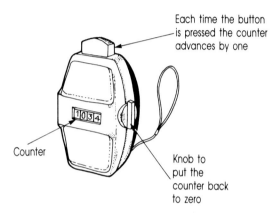

A hand tally counter

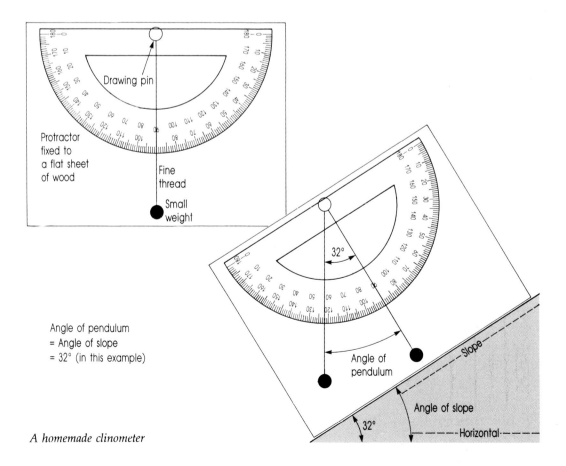

A homemade clinometer

Different types of vehicle in London's Piccadilly

A traffic census

Several different types of traffic census can be undertaken on most roads, such as:

- a survey of all the vehicles passing the observation point in one (or both) directions;

- a survey of all the vehicles passing the observation point but classifying them according to the different types of vehicle, such as lorries, vans, cars, cycles, motor bikes;

- a survey of the destination of the vehicles taking different exits at a road junction (you will need the assistance of several friends in order to do this unless the roads are little used);

- a survey of the places of origin of the different vehicles passing the observation point (use the registration letters indicating the place of registration and the names of towns printed on the sides of commercial vehicles);

- a survey of the number of pedestrians using the different streets in the centre of town (including pedestrian precincts and shopping centres).

Consider whether you should make several traffic counts:

- at different times of day, such as the morning and evening rush hours, midday, etc.;

- on different days of the week, such as market day, early closing day, weekends;

- at different times of the year, such as in winter and in summer.

Plot the results of your traffic count(s) on a map or on a graph like those below and opposite. Notice how the width of the bars on the map has been drawn to scale to indicate the importance of each route. Other graphs which you could use are listed on pages 77–80.

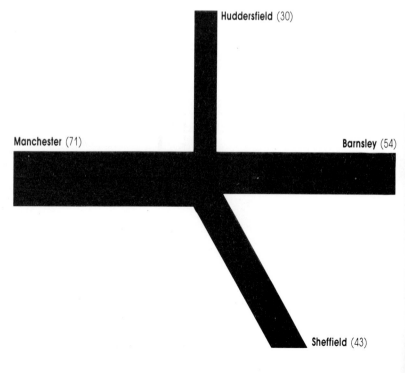

A star graph showing differing volumes of traffic at a road junction

Towns of origin of lorries passing through Penistone (near Sheffield) during a period of 90 minutes

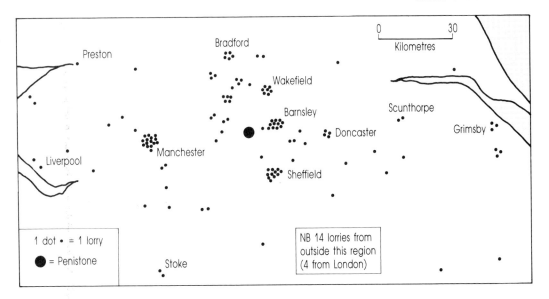

Measuring amenities

The simplest way to assess the usefulness of a public amenity, such as a shopping centre or railway station, is to measure the distance from that amenity to a residential area or to the town centre.

Suppose you wish to measure how accessible the main shopping centre is to the people travelling into your nearest town. You have identified the main points where the majority of shoppers disembark as being the bus station, railway station, and three town centre car parks.

1 Select three department stores or chain stores which you regard as being among the most important shops in the town.

2 Plot these stores on a tracing of a map of the town centre and draw lines to join them up to form a triangle.

3 Measure the distance *in paces* from one of the sides of this triangle to each of the main car parks, and to the bus and railway stations.

4 Record your measurements in a table like the one below.

5 Which is the most convenient way of travelling into the town to shop?

6 Do the car park charges vary with distance from the triangle? If not, why not?

Distance to the main triangle (Marks & Spencer, Debenhams, W H Smith)

From	Distance (in paces)	Time taken on foot (in minutes)	Comments
Railway station	1230	14	Inconvenient – uphill all the way
Bus station	90	Under 1	Very convenient
Multi-storey car park	170	2	Excellent – the most convenient car park
Short stay car park	315	4	Convenient but uphill most of the way and few shops en route
Long stay car park	790	9	Some distance from the main triangle but many shops en route

An amenity index

The attractiveness of one place in which to live compared with another is usually a matter of opinion and judgement. It cannot be measured easily. However, it is possible to compare places by rating them according to the services they offer the people living there. This is called an *amenity index*.

It is constructed by awarding a rating of so many points depending on whether a particular service is available locally and on its distance from the place in question. Thus a maximum rating of 5 points might be awarded if a home is within 5 minutes walking distance of a supermarket, 4 points if within 5 to 10 minutes, 3 points if within 10 to 20 minutes, 2 points within 20 minutes to 40 minutes, and only 1 point if more than 40 minutes away.

Different people have different ideas as to what would, or would not, be considered an amenity. In the amenity index below, you can see a comparison between a house on the outskirts of a small country market town in Suffolk, a farmhouse in a hamlet in Northumberland and a flat in a London borough:

Under 5 minutes	5 points
5–10 minutes	4 points
10–20 minutes	3 points
20–40 minutes	2 points
Over 40 minutes	1 point

Amenity	Suffolk market town	Northumberland farmhouse	Flat in London borough
Post box	5	3	5
Telephone box	5	3	5
Post office	3	1	5
Bus stop	5	1	5
Primary school	4	1	5
Secondary school	4	1	4
Place of work	5	5	2
Place of worship	3	3	4
Supermarket	4	1	5
Newsagent	3	2	5
Department store	1	1	3
Woolworths	3	1	3
Public house	4	3	5
Cinema	3	1	4
Theatre	1	1	2
Swimming pool	4	1	4
Public park	5	1	5
Railway station	3	1	4
Dentist	3	1	4
Doctor	4	1	5
Total (max. = 100)	72	33	84

Note: The maximum (the total number of amenities multiplied by the maximum number of points for each amenity) is $20 \times 5 = 100$.

EXERCISES

1. How might a tally counter and a simple clinometer be useful if you were making:
   a) a comparison between two beaches?
   b) a comparison between two farms?

2. Construct a resort index which can be used to compare the merits of one seaside resort with another.

Field sketching and field mapping

Some fieldwork information can be shown on a *field sketch* or in a *field map* drawn roughly to scale. The main difference between them is that a sketch of a feature shows what it looks like on the ground, whilst the map shows what it looks like from immediately above (see page 37). You do not have to be an artist to draw a passable field sketch. Nor do you have to be a skilled surveyor and cartographer to draw a good field map.

You do, however, need to be neat and tidy, to be patient, and have the right tools to do the job – a pencil, a sharpener, and a pen with a fine nib or ballpoint to write neat labels.

The first thing to do is to decide whether a field sketch or a field map will add anything to the information you have already found out about a subject. Can you show something on a drawing or on a map which cannot be shown in any other way?

Bear in mind that there is no point in drawing a field sketch just for the sake of it. A photograph will almost certainly be more accurate. But a field sketch or field map can be an effective way of showing the size and shape of a building or of a geographical feature, such as a meander (often difficult to photograph).

You can also use a field map or field sketch to show the links between physical features and the ways in which human beings have used the environment. This can be shown on a pair of field sketches like those on page 36 illustrating the physical and human geography of a small area in Scotland.

EXERCISES

1 **Look closely at the field sketches of Farr Bay, Scotland on page 36. How do the second and third field sketches differ from each other? How are they similar? How do they complement each other?**

2 **How has physical geography affected the land use of this area? How have humans altered the land?**

Field sketches

1 Sketch in the broad outline of the feature. If you do this in pencil you can rub it out if you are not satisfied with your first try. At all times keep your sketch as simple and as neat as possible. (In the example you can see the different stages involved in drawing a field sketch of a roche moutonnée – a small rock shaped and scratched by ice action.)

2 Add the details which you think are important, such as the striations shown in the field sketch below. These are scratches which were made by ice as it scraped the surface of bare rock.

3 Add shading to show the slope of the land (if this is relevant).

4 Label your field sketch noting down carefully any measurements you may have taken.

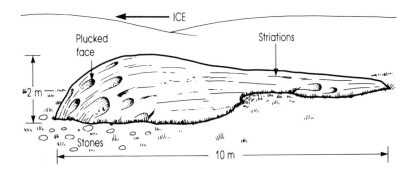

If you do decide to draw a field sketch, only include the details which you think are relevant to your project. You can see how this is done in the field sketches on this page. See how the same sketch has been used for both drawings. The first shows information about the physical features in the bay. The second sketch shows how the bay is used by the people who live there.

Preliminary field sketch of Farr Bay, Scotland

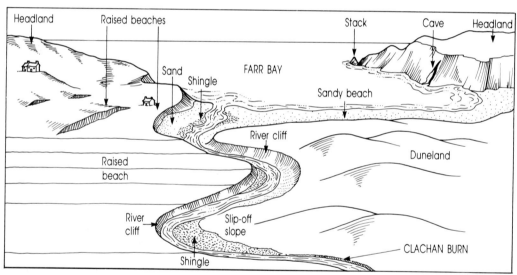

Field sketch of Farr Bay, Scotland to show its main physical features

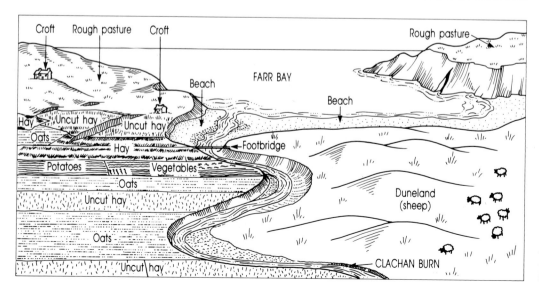

Field sketch of Farr Bay, Scotland showing land use

Field maps

This field map of a river meander was drawn by estimating the width of the river and by pacing out the section to be mapped. An outline was sketched in light pencil and amended with the aid of an eraser until a satisfactory map had been drawn.

The outline was inked in and labelled with the rough measurements. Then the different types of deposit in the river bed were named and marked on the map.

Sometimes it makes sense to draw both a field map and a field sketch. This is illustrated by the field maps (below) of the roche moutonnée which was shown earlier on page 35. What can a field map show that cannot be shown in a field sketch?

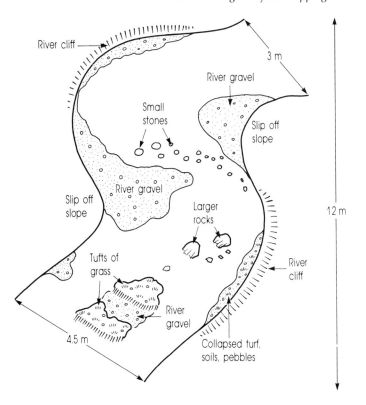

Field map to show the deposits in a river bed at a meander

Method

1. Draw the map outline roughly to scale.

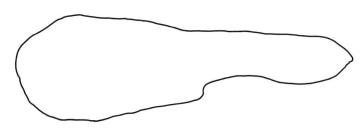

2. Locate the main details carefully.

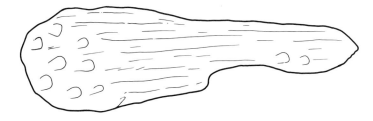

3. Add measurements and labels.

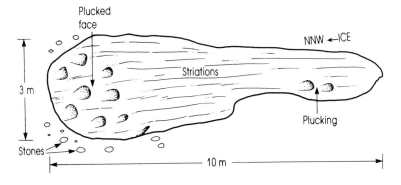

EXERCISES

1. Draw a field sketch of the photograph of the Fort William area on page 57. Sketch in the outline carefully and label it to show the aluminium works in the foreground (right), the River Lochy (right), Loch Linnhe (centre) and the town of Fort William (left).

2. Draw a field sketch of your school and annotate it to draw attention to its main features.

3. Draw a quick field map of a room in a building, such as your classroom, or a room at home. Pace out or estimate the measurements. Draw the map roughly to scale. Mark in, and label neatly, the more important features, such as desks, bookshelves, and tables.

4. Draw a field sketch and field map of some geographical feature close to your home or school, such as a factory, river, farm, part of a river valley, beach, city centre or suburban shopping centre. Show on the field map features which cannot be shown on the field sketch, and vice versa.

A flow diagram

Another useful technique you can sometimes use is that of the flow diagram. This is simply a diagram to represent how things move on the ground, such as how raw materials are processed in a factory or how goods are shipped overseas in containers. Its great advantage in geographical fieldwork is that it can often be used to explain and simplify an otherwise complicated process. In the example below you can see how a flow diagram has been drawn to show how herrings are traditionally processed in a kippering kiln.

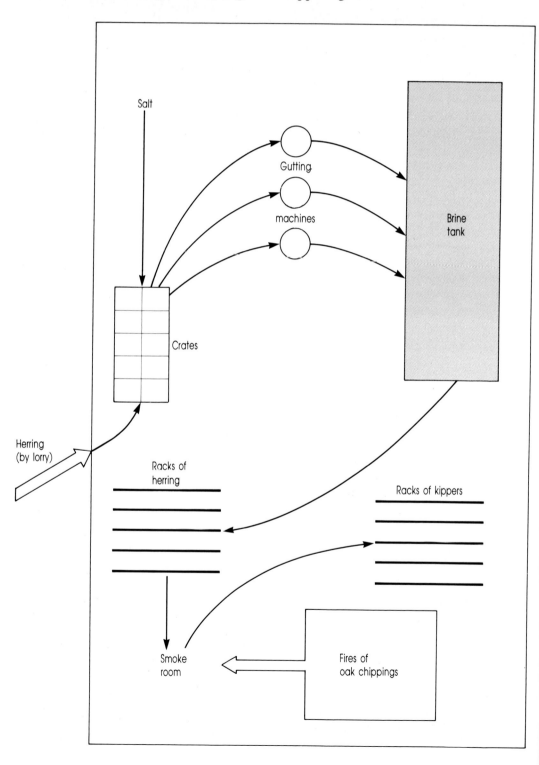

Flow diagram of a kippering kiln

Maps in geographical fieldwork

The essential tool in geographical fieldwork is the *map*. As you have seen (page 37) it can show clearly and exactly the relationship of things or places to each other on the ground. It is a form of shorthand, telling us about the land and about the ways in which people have used and are using that land.

Much of the information you find out about in the course of your fieldwork can be shown on a map, either on a field map (see page 37) or on a large-scale Ordnance Survey map (pages 56 and 58).

You can see how the same base map can be used again and again in the maps on this page. Here a field map of a small part of a town has been used in six different ways:

A *annotated* with descriptions of different types of building;

B as a *dot distribution map* showing the extent to which brick buildings dominate the area;

C with *symbols* marking the position of different types of housing;

D marked with *abbreviations* summing up the principal house types in the area;

E *shaded or coloured* to show the ages of the buildings in the area;

F with *numbers* indicating the number of storeys in each building.

Base maps like these can later be used in the classroom as the raw material for more carefully drawn maps presenting your fieldwork information neatly and precisely.

EXERCISES

1 What do the maps tell you about the houses in this part of town?

2 What are the disadvantages of Map A?

3 Which do you think are the easiest maps to understand at a glance?

4 Which map crams a lot of information into a small space? Is it easy to understand at a glance?

5 Which maps show the same pattern, even though they use different data with different symbols?

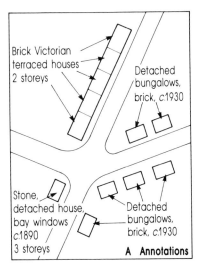

A Annotations

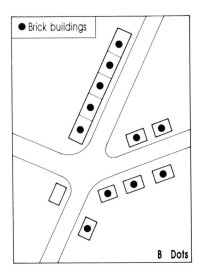

B Dots

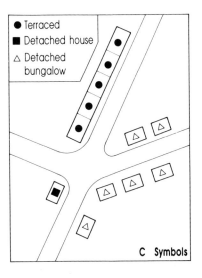

C Symbols

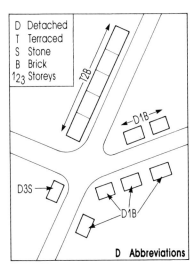

D Abbreviations

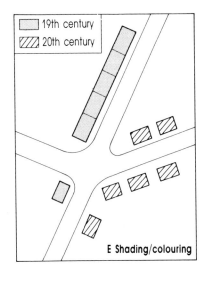

E Shading/colouring

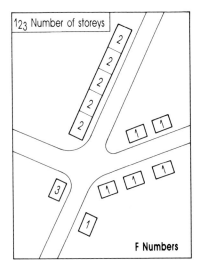

F Numbers

A land-use map

The use made of the land, such as the different types of farmland and the different uses to which land is put in a town (industry, business, shopping, recreation, etc.) can best be studied if you conduct a land-use survey first of all.

To do this you will need to prepare a base map on which to record information using symbols, colours, abbreviations, or annotations like those shown in the maps on page 39. If there is sufficient space on the map it is probably best to write out in full the type of land use you see there. This avoids any later confusion between P for park or P for car park, peas, or potatoes!

In the examples opposite you can see three stages in the construction of a land-use map of a farm:

1 The base map shows the outlines of the fields, areas of woodland, roads, buildings, etc. The choice of scale for the base map will depend largely on the maps available to you at school. Be prepared to add details, such as buildings, to the map since these may have been built since the map was last surveyed or revised. If you copy the map in the classroom keep it as simple as possible. Some of the information on the printed map will be irrelevant to your study.

2 The annotated field map uses the minimum of symbols. In a town you will probably have to use letters, numbers, abbreviations, colours, and signs because so many different types of land use are often encountered in a small area.

3 The completed land-use map, using different types of shading, symbol, or colour, shows you immediately the major categories of land use (such as woodland and arable land). Use a standard system of classifying the different types of land use like the one below:

Arable
Permanent grassland
Orchards
Market gardening
Heath, moorland, rough pasture
Industry
Urban
Woodland
Water and water features

EXERCISES

1 What does this land-use map tell you about the farm?

2 What do you notice about the distribution of arable land on this farm?

Urban land use, Huddersfield

A land-use map

Land-use map of a mixed farm in Northumberland

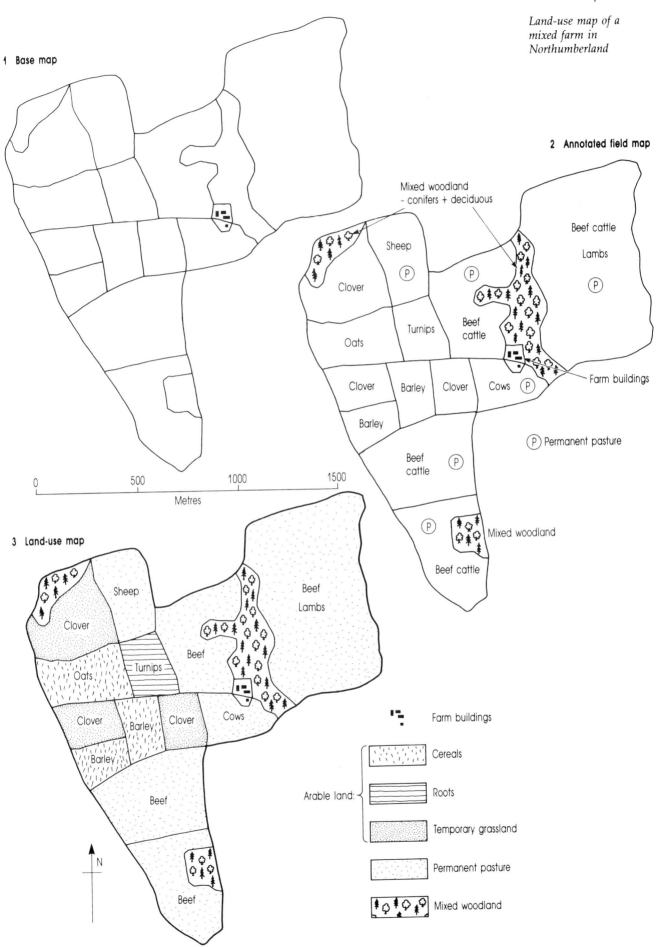

Photographs and tape recordings

Some of the information you acquire during the course of a field study need not necessarily be recorded by pen on paper. A good photograph can be every bit as informative as a field sketch. Cassette recorders can help you when you conduct a series of interviews asking people to answer questions in questionnaires.

However, photographs and cassette recordings are only useful ways of recording information if they add to the results of your fieldwork and are not simply used to illustrate what you have already found out from other sources.

There is no great secret about taking effective photographs. The most important thing is to ensure that the photographs are correctly exposed and correctly focused.

Graffiti in Sheffield. Some topics are better illustrated with photographs than with maps or sketches. Can you think of a better way of demonstrating the problem of pollution in towns?

Scrap heap in south London

Dereliction in Liverpool

Polluted river in Teesside

EXERCISES

1. What other fieldwork topics in geography do you think are better illustrated by the camera than by the pencil?

2. How can photographs and cassette recordings be of value when studying:
   a) rivers and valleys?   c) transport?
   b) seaside resorts?

Interviews and questionnaires

Many surveys can be undertaken in a town if you are prepared to interview shoppers and passers-by. You can only do this successfully if you are polite and very patient. The people you approach may not understand what you are trying to do. So each time you approach someone you will have to explain what you are doing and seek their co-operation. Some of the people you approach will be too busy to spend time answering your questions. So be prepared!

Try to develop a technique of interviewing that will help you to get the maximum amount of information without wasting the time of the person you are interviewing. If you use a cassette recorder to record your interviews ask permission first and then try to ensure that the position of the recorder is not too obvious. Many people are put off by the idea that their voice is being recorded.

Make sure you have a list of questions ready. Do not go up to farmers with a vague enquiry asking them to tell you something about their farms. Be more specific. Why do they keep dairy herds? Why do they grow cereals? How important is the climate in deciding which type of farming to follow?

You will often find it useful if you prepare a standard questionnaire so that you can ask each person the same questions and put down their answers in the same order each time. This will make analysis of the results of your survey much easier to undertake.

You will find it easier to carry out your survey if you make multiple copies of your questionnaire first. You may be able to do this on a photocopier at school. If not, use the one in your local library. You can speed up the process by making a photocopy of your questionnaire on to A4 paper first of all. Then place this photocopy next to your original and photocopy both together on to A3 paper.

Suppose you are investigating the hypothesis that most of the shoppers using a suburban shopping centre are local people who have travelled there by car from places less than five kilometres (three miles) away. Prepare a preliminary draft of a questionnaire to help you test this hypothesis:

- How do the shoppers travel to the shopping centre?
- Is that their usual way of getting to the shopping centre?
- How far have they travelled from their homes?
- How frequently do they use the shopping centre?
- What other shopping centres do they use like this and how many times a week (or month)?

When drafting a questionnaire bear in mind the methods you will later use to sort out the answers. You may think it will be useful to see if there is any difference in the responses you get from people of different ages or from different sexes. Leave space on the questionnaire to insert details of this type after you have interviewed each shopper. Do not ask people to their face for personal details like this. Many people would think you were being very rude if you directly asked them their age!

When you have drafted your questionnaire try it out first on your friends and relatives before seeking the approval of your teacher. Testing out your questions thoroughly in advance is the best way to get rid of mistakes and to avoid questions which people may later find rude or difficult to answer.

When you have completed your survey of shoppers analyse the completed questionnaires. You will be able to use a number of different ways of analysing the statistics (see pages 81–5) and you will also have several choices when it comes to preparing graphs from these statistics (see pages 77–80).

EXERCISE

Draft a short questionnaire to find out which type of shop the people of your area would most like to see opened in your nearest town in the immediate future.

Studying the evidence

When you have completed your fieldwork you will have to consider how you can best present your evidence as part of a convincing enquiry.

You will need to study the evidence you have collected very carefully indeed. Can you see any pattern in the data you have collected? Are there any patterns in the maps or graphs you have drawn? Do they satisfactorily prove or disprove the assertion or hypothesis you set out to examine in the first place?

Ideally your project will have:

- an interesting beginning, stating clearly the aims and objectives of your study, so that the examiner can see what it is you set out to study, test, prove, or disprove.

- an explanation of the data you set out to collect in order to achieve the aims and objectives outlined at the start of your study.

- a conclusion summing up the results of your fieldwork clearly and logically.

The examiners of your fieldwork enquiry will expect you to be able to show:

- that you have used original first-hand sources for much of your work, such as fieldwork data, printed evidence and statistics, large-scale Ordnance Survey maps, photographs, responses to questionnaires, etc.

- that you have carefully selected only the evidence and conclusions which are relevant to the topics you are studying.

- that your conclusions are based on facts you have studied at first-hand rather than on ideas and facts you have read about in books.

- that you have experienced in detail the techniques and methods you used to observe, obtain, collect, and record data.

- that you have also explained any difficulties you may have encountered and any possible defects or deficiencies in the data.

- that you have shown yourself capable of using different skills in your enquiry:
  - Your enquiry will be expected to contain accurate maps, diagrams, graphs, charts, photographs, and field sketches if these are relevant and appropriate to the enquiry.
  - You will need to label, annotate, or caption accurately these maps, graphs, photographs, and sketches and relate them in the written part of your study to the aims and objectives of your fieldwork as a whole.
  - Maps should always carry scales and map legends or keys to explain the symbols and abbreviations used on the map.
  - Graphs should always be clearly labelled to indicate what data has been used and how it has been plotted on the graph.
  - If you use statistics, make sure they are relevant, presented clearly and that you indicate how they were collected or obtained.
  - Tables of statistics should be accurately labelled to make it absolutely clear what the numbers in each column and in each row represent.
  - If you talk about averages, make sure you use the correct terms – mean, median and mode.

- that you know how to present your findings in a form which can be easily understood by the reader:
  - Number the pages of your enquiry and make sure that the reader can always relate the diagrams, graphs, maps, and photographs to the text.
  - You may also be required to provide a list of contents, an index, a list of acknowledgements, and a list of books, newspapers, maps, etc., which you have used during the course of your study. This is called a bibliography.

Skills in geography

As you can see, there are a number of different skills which you will have to employ when you carry out your fieldwork investigations. They are illustrated in the diagram below.

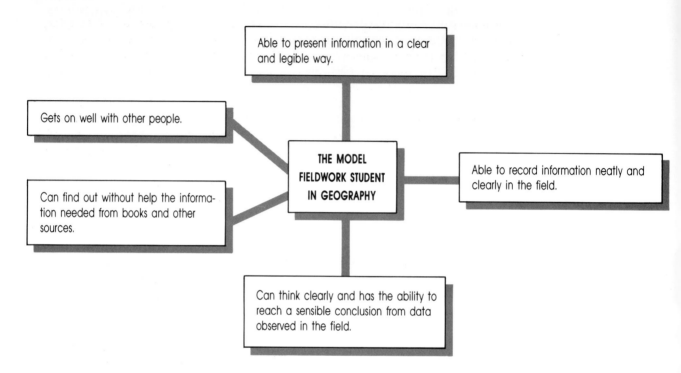

USING MAPS AND PHOTOGRAPHS

Mapwork

The Ordnance Survey is responsible for the surveying and mapping of Great Britain. The department issues maps at different scales. The maps you are most likely to encounter are those issued on the 1:1250, 1:2500, 1:10 000, 1:25 000, 1:50 000, and 1:250 000 map scales.

Symbols, signs, colours, and abbreviations are used to show much of the information on these maps. The legends, or keys, of the most commonly used maps, the 1:25 000 and 1:50 000 series, are shown on pages 54 and 55.

We also use many other types of maps. Large-scale foreign maps, street plans, road maps, atlas maps, maps provided by estate agents, newspaper and television maps, 'you are here' maps in public places, underground and bus route maps, 'how to get to my home' maps, and many others are used every day at home, at work, on the road, and on holiday. Many of these maps will be useful to you in your fieldwork and mapwork enquiries.

The maps on this page and page 48 have been chosen to show the differences the scale makes to the way in which information is depicted on a map (see also page 53). Which map you choose for a particular task depends largely on the scale. As you can see, the larger the scale (i.e. the 1:1250 and 1:2500 maps), the greater the amount of detail which can be shown but the smaller the land area covered by the map. The smaller the scale (i.e. 1:25 000), the greater the extent of the land area covered by the map, the less the detail it can show.

1:1250 map scale
Crown copyright reserved

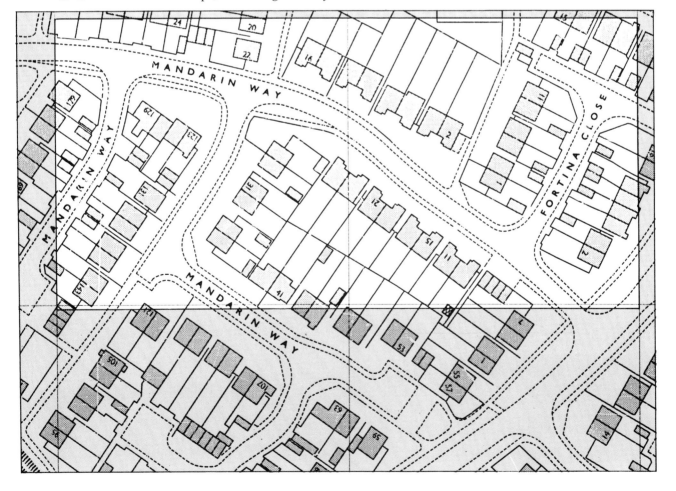

EXERCISES

Look closely at the maps on this page and page 47.

1. What are the main differences between a map on the 1:1250 scale and those on the other scales?

2. Which map scale would you choose to show:
   a) the position of a golf course in relation to a town?
   b) the position of the schools, shops, and meeting places within 10 minutes walk of a block of flats?
   c) the exact size of a building?

3. Which is the more recent map here – the 1:1250 or the 1:2500?

1:25 000 map scale
Crown copyright reserved

1:10 000 map scale
Crown copyright reserved

1:2500 map scale
Crown copyright reserved

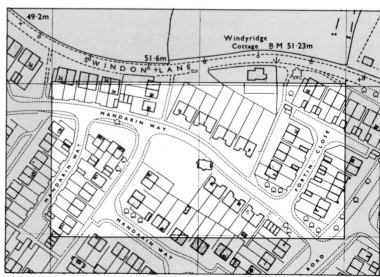

Essential Tools for Mapwork

Sharp pencil and pen
Graph paper (2 mm squares)
Geometrical compass
Fine tracing paper
Magnetic compass
Magnifying lens
Scrap paper
30 cm ruler
Protractor

Scales and measurements

Most of the maps and plans you will use are drawn to *scale*. The scale of the map is usually shown by one or more of these three main methods:

- *A simple statement of the map scale,* such as 1 centimetre equals 1 kilometre.

- *A representative fraction* expressing the ratio between a single unit of length on the map and the actual distance that that single unit of length represents on the ground such as 1:1250, 1:2500, 1:10 000, 1:25 000 or 1:50 000.

  For instance, on the 1:50 000 map scale, a length of 1 millimetre on the map represents 50 000 millimetres on the ground (i.e. 50 metres). A length of 1 centimetre on the map represents 50 000 centimetres on the ground (i.e. 500 metres or 0.5 kilometres).

  The ratio 1:50 000 always remains the same irrespective of the unit of length. Thus 1 inch = 50 000 inches, 1 foot = 50 000 feet, 1 Martian mile = 50 000 Martian miles! It is called a representative fraction because the ratio can also be expressed as a fraction, such as $\frac{1}{50\,000}$, $\frac{1}{25\,000}$, $\frac{1}{10\,000}$, and so on. This means that on the 1:50 000 map any distance on the map is $\frac{1}{50\,000}$th the length of its actual distance on the ground.

- *A linear scale.* This is a line on the map which has been graduated (divided) into smaller sections, each section representing an equal distance on the map. On the 1:50 000 map, a distance of 10 centimetres represents $10 \times 50\,000$ centimetres on the map. This is a distance of 500 000 centimetres = 5000 metres = 5 kilometres. So a linear scale on the 1:50 000 map scale could be drawn by ruling a line 10 centimetres long and marking it off with five equal 2-centimetre intervals and labelling them 1, 2, 3, 4, 5 kilometres respectively.

Straight-line distances on a map can be measured with a straight-edged piece of paper. Place it between the two points on the map and mark off their position with a sharp pencil. Place the edge against the linear scale and simply read off the actual distance on the ground.

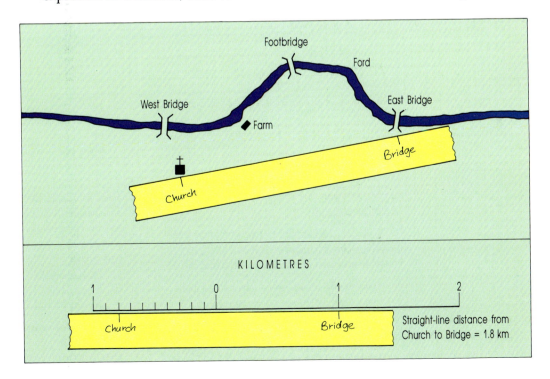

Curving distances, such as those following a road, coastline, or river, are more complicated but can be measured by dividing the route into straight sections, *or* by using thin thread carefully shaped so that it follows the bends in the route, *or* by using a map measure (opisometer).

The same principles apply whatever the maps you use, whether on the 1:50 000, 1:25 000, 1:10 000, 1:2500, or 1:1250 map scales.

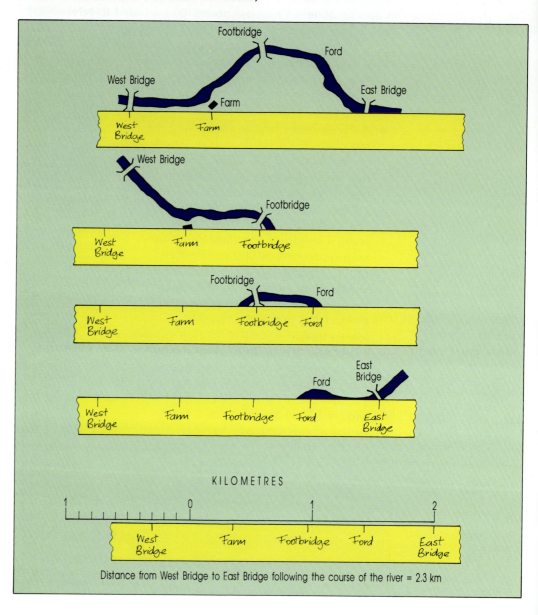

Distance from West Bridge to East Bridge following the course of the river = 2.3 km

EXERCISES

Look at the 1:50 000 Ordnance Survey map on page 56.

1. What is the straight-line distance between the Mountain Rescue Post in Fort William and the summit of Cow Hill?

2. How far is it by ferry across the loch from Fort William to Camusnagaul?

3. How far is it from the summit of Ben Nevis in a straight line westwards to the motel on the shore of the loch?

4. How far is it from the pier near the Mountain Rescue Post in Fort William to the lighthouse (shown by a small picture of a lighthouse) in Corpach to the north
   a) in a straight line by boat?
   b) by railway (the thick black line)?
   c) by main road (shown in red)?

5. What is the width of a grid square
   (a) in metres?
   (b) in kilometres?

Directions on a map

In geography you will often need to locate one place in relation to another. For most purposes this can be done simply by indicating the compass direction.

The top of a map usually points north. The only exceptions to this occur if it is more convenient or more logical (usually because of the shape of the area covered) to have some other compass point at the top of the map. On Ordnance Survey maps the grid lines point to *grid north* (which is nearly but not exactly the same as *true north*). To make matters more complicated the north found by a compass is *magnetic north* and this is not true north either! It varies slightly from year to year. You can work out by how much if you look at the compass information given on the map.

For most purposes it is usually sufficient to use the 16 main compass points, north, north-north-east, north-east, etc., to describe the relationship between places. You can see these sixteen compass points (abbreviated to NNE, NE, etc.) in the diagram below.

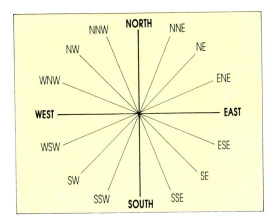

In the map below the church is north *of* the school, whilst *from* the school the bus station is due south. Note that it is essential that you know *from* which point the direction is to be measured.

EXERCISES

Look at the map on this page.

1 What direction is the abbey from the school?

2 What direction is the school from the wood?

3 What direction is the school from the bridge?

4 What lies SSE of the abbey?

5 What lies ESE of the school?

6 In which corner of the map is the lake situated?

Look at the Ordnance Survey map on page 56.

7 What is the direction of the lighthouse in Corpach from the Aluminium Works in the centre of the map?

8 In which part of the map area are the pulp and paper mills (near Corpach) situated?

9 Find Inverlochy Castle (NE of Fort William and E from the Pulp and Paper Mills). In which direction would

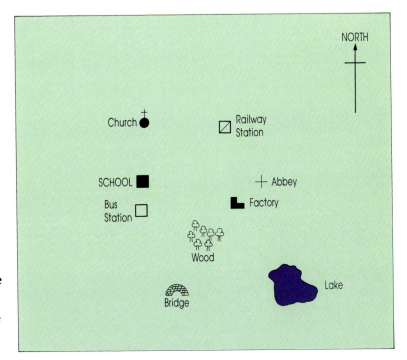

you have to face if you wanted to look from the castle towards the summit of Ben Nevis?

10 In which direction would you travel if you caught the ferry from Camusnagaul to Fort William?

Grid references

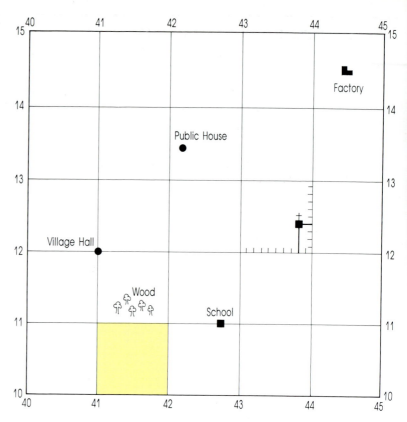

All Ordnance Survey maps use the National Grid. This is a network of squares within squares which covers the whole of Great Britain. The largest squares (100 km × 100 km) can be identified by their two-letter references, such as TQ in the London region, TM in Suffolk, and NT around Edinburgh.

Within each large grid square there are one hundred smaller squares each covering an area of 10 km by 10 km. Each of these squares can be identified by the grid lines which form the southern and western sides of the square. As you can see from the diagram below, these grid lines are numbered so that they increase in size from 0 to 9 as you travel east (called the *Eastings*) and likewise from 0 to 9 as you travel north (called the *Northings*). The grid square 75 is, therefore, identified first by the Easting (7) and then by the Northing (5). The intersection 75 is where the two grid lines cross and this is the south-western corner of the square.

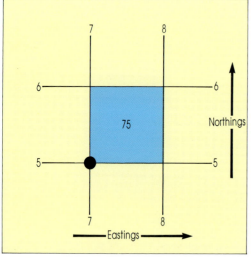

Each of these large grid squares is further sub-divided into 100 smaller squares, 1 km by 1 km in size. These kilometre squares can also be identified, by a four-digit grid reference number, calculated in the same way as the two-digit number. Thus the shaded square in the map above right is first identified by the Easting 41 and then by the Northing 10. So the four-digit grid reference for the shaded square is 4110.

Even this is not sufficiently detailed to identify a feature such as a church tower or a post office. This is why the position of a feature on an Ordnance Survey map, such as the church, is almost always identified by a six-digit grid reference number, such as 438124. As you can see, the easting is 43 but the position of the church tower is on an imaginary grid line eight-tenths of the distance between the 43 and 44 Eastings. So we say its position is identified by the Easting 43 8. Similarly its position is also four-tenths of the distance between the 12 and 13 Northings. So we say its Northing is 12 4. The full grid reference is, therefore, 438124.

Note that on the 1:25 000 map series the edge of the map is already divided into tenths to help you find these six-figure grid references quickly.

If you use the two grid letters as well as the six-figure grid reference, you can give each place in Britain a unique grid reference. For instance, the reference SP 180451 identifies the position of a barn in the Cotswolds. The two letters (SP) identify the 100 km square of the National Grid, whilst the six-digit reference identifies a square 100 m × 100 m on that map.

FINDING A SIX-FIGURE GRID REFERENCE

1. Locate the number of the *Easting* grid line (first two digits) which runs vertically from top to bottom down the map.

2. The third digit in the grid reference gives the position of an imaginary grid line so many tenths of the way between the two grid lines on the map.

3. Run your finger, or a pointer, so many tenths eastwards from the Easting grid line until you fix this position.

4. Do the same thing with the last three digits in the grid reference.
   The fourth and fifth digits give the number of the *Northing* grid line running from side to side across the map. The sixth digit gives the position of an imaginary grid line so many tenths north of the Northing grid line.

EXERCISES

Look at the map opposite.

1. What is the four-digit grid reference for the square in which the church is situated? In which grid square would you see a wood?

2. Give the six-digit grid reference for:
   a) the public house;
   b) the village hall.

3. What would you expect to see at 445145 and at 427110?

Look at the Ordnance Survey map on page 56.

4. What would you expect to see at 099739, 105762, 140778?

5. What would you expect to see in grid squares 1173, 1376, 0772?

6. Give six-figure grid references for the Mountain Rescue Posts:
   a) in Fort William;
   b) on Ben Nevis;
   and the caravan sites in grid squares:
   c) 0777;
   d) 1276.

Points, patches, lines, symbols and abbreviations

On very large scale maps or plans, such as the Ordnance Survey 1:1250 and 1:2500 series, it is possible to reproduce buildings and roads exactly to scale. On smaller scale maps, however, mapmakers usually have to use points, lines and patches. These points, lines, and patches can be identified on most maps by reference to a panel attached to the map, called the *map key* or *map legend*.

- *Points* are used (such as a cross for a chapel and a small symbol to show a windmill) to identify features whose position can be identified by a single grid reference.

- Features which are identified by their extent or area (such as woodland, lakes, sandy beaches, marshland, and rough pasture) are usually shown as *patches* of colour, or as shaded areas, on the map. They are sometimes identified by the addition of a *symbol* as well, such as the small trees shown as woodland on the 1:25 000 map series.

- Linear features which have length and little breadth are shown as different coloured *lines* often varying in thickness according to their importance, such as a canal, river, power line, railway, and main road.

- *Abbreviations* (such as PH for Public House and T for Telephone) are used to identify specific features on the map.

You will find mapwork much easier if you can master the keys to the two main map series, the 1:50 000 series on pages 54–5 and the 1:25 000 series on page 55.

Skills: Using Maps and Photographs

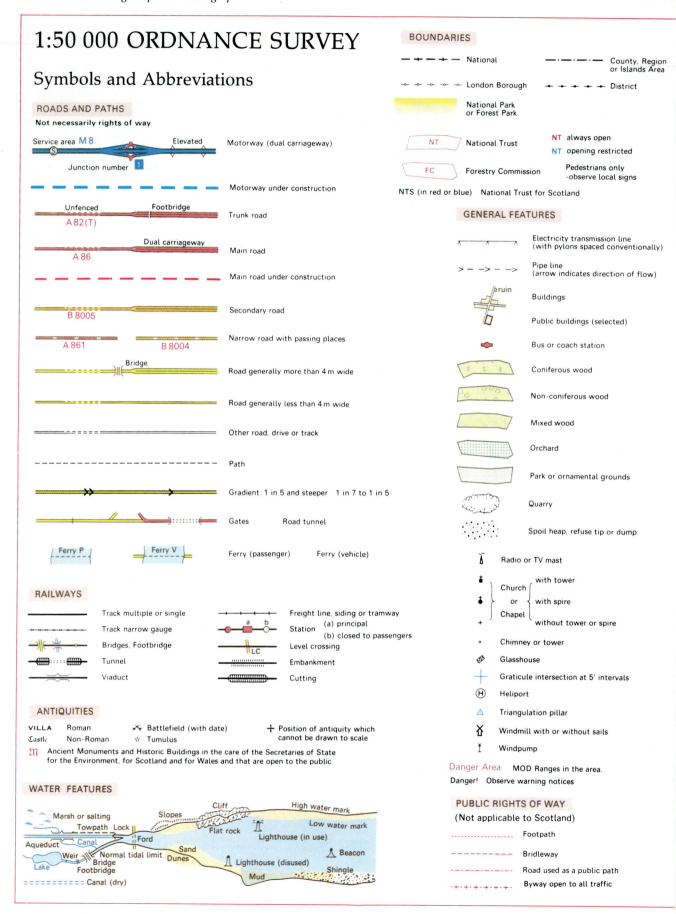

Reproduced from an Ordnance Survey 1:50 000 map with the permission of the Controller of Her Majesty's Stationery Office, Crown copyright reserved.

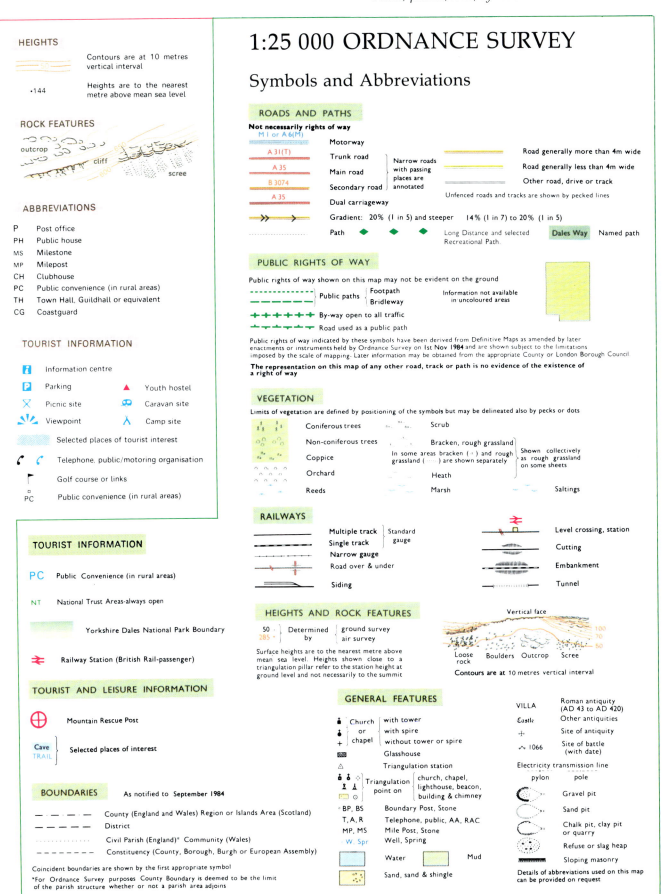

ORDNANCE SURVEY MAP EXTRACT 1:50 000 SERIES: FORT WILLIAM

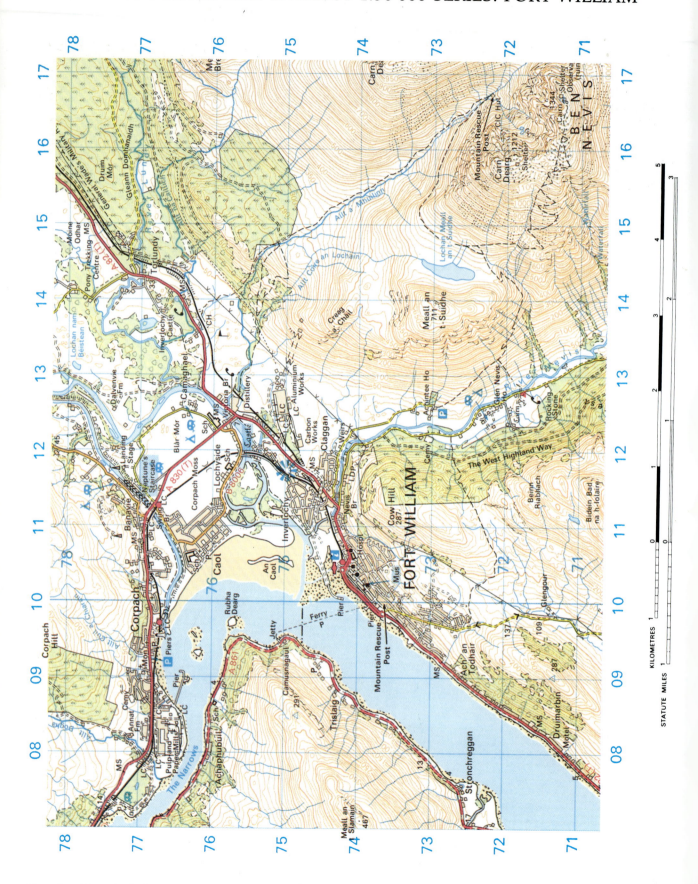

Reproduced from the Ordnance Survey map 1:50 000 Landranger 41 with the permission of the Controller of Her Majesty's Stationery Office, Crown copyright reserved.

Points, patches, lines, symbols and abbreviations 57

Aerial photograph of part of the Fort William area shown on the map opposite

ORDNANCE SURVEY MAP EXTRACT 1:25 000 SERIES: INGLETON

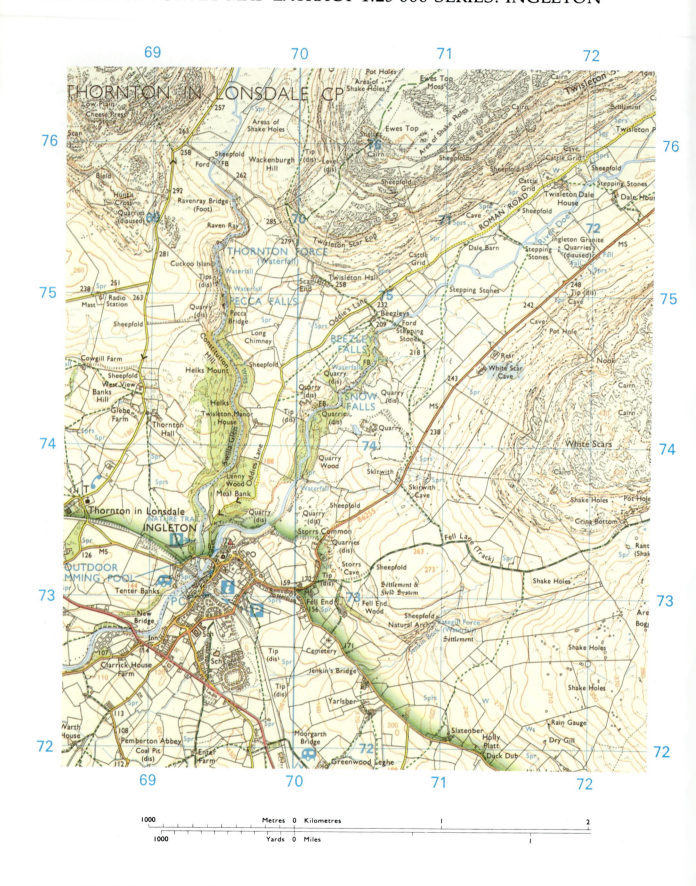

Reproduced from the Ordnance Survey Map 1:25 000 Outdoor Leisure 2 with the permission of the Controller of Her Majesty's Stationery Office, Crown copyright reserved.

Aerial photograph of part of the Ingleton area shown on the map opposite

Maps and photographs

Relating a map to a photograph is not as simple a task as it sounds. This is partly because the only photographs which can show exactly what is on the map are aerial photographs taken from immediately above the ground. These are called *vertical* aerial photographs. Not surprisingly, they look more like maps than photographs, as you can see from the photograph on page 63 which shows central London and the River Thames. Vertical aerial photographs are usually more difficult to understand than large-scale maps of the same area, since they do not have symbols and abbreviations to identify the features shown in them.

Pictures taken from the air at an angle are called *oblique* aerial photographs. The oblique aerial photograph looking up the River Thames on page 62 shows part of the area covered by the vertical photograph facing it on page 63. Exercises 12–18 opposite will help you to relate the two photographs to each other and to a map of Central London (if you can find one in the road atlas).

The view taken in by the camera lens is like that seen by the human eye. It takes in an *angle of view*. So photographs taken from an angle, whether from the air or on the ground, always show an angle of view which does not correspond to a square or rectangle on a map. You see the features in the foreground in detailed close-up, though they are often only a few metres across. By contrast, features on the horizon may be several kilometres wide.

What you see on a photograph also depends partly on the focal length of the camera lens. A telephoto lens works like a telescope. It has a long focal length and a narrow angle of view, while a wide-angle lens has a short focal length and a wide angle of view. It also depends upon whether the lens is focused to make features in the foreground sharp (and those in the distance blurred) or features in the distance sharp (and those in close-up blurred). Needless to say, it also depends on whether a feature in the foreground obscures a feature on the horizon, such as a tree or a small hill hiding the summit of a mountain.

In working out the angle of view revealed by the camera bear in mind that all the features depicted close to the left-hand side of the photograph must lie on a straight line on the map. The same thing is true of the right-hand side of the photograph. You can use this fact to work out where the photograph was taken, since by identifying two or more features on or close to the edge of each side of the photograph you will be able to find two converging lines on the map. The photograph was taken from the point where the two lines meet.

HOW TO WORK OUT AN ANGLE OF VIEW

1. Look first to see if there is an easily recognisable linear feature, such as the winding course of a river, road, railway, power line, or canal. The length of the linear feature and its direction could soon help you to find the general area covered on both the photograph and on the map.

2. Try to find landmarks which cannot be easily mistaken, such as a church tower or spire, a patch of woodland, an island, a lake, an isolated farmhouse, a bridge or viaduct, etc. Line these features up on the map with the features you can see on the photograph.

3. Once you have identified the approximate position of the camera you can then line it up precisely by matching the features on the left- and right-hand sides of the photograph with their counterparts on the map.

EXERCISES

Look at the map of Fort William on page 56 and at the facing aerial photograph on page 57.

1. Find the approximate position of the camera when the photograph was taken. *Clue:* Line up the pier in Fort William with the road on the *left* and the canal at Banavie with the Victoria Bridge on the *right*.
2. In which direction was the camera pointing?
3. What is the name of the hill in the top left-hand corner of the photograph? What is its height above sea level?
4. What type of factory is shown in the bottom right-hand corner of the photograph?
5. Identify the following features on both the map and the photograph:
   a) the position of a castle
   b) the island of Rubha Dearg
   c) Corpach Moss
   d) the river Lochy
   e) the village of Caol
   f) the island of An Caol.
6. Trace the photograph and then mark on your tracing the position of:
   a) Claggan
   b) the A82 trunk road
   c) a pulp and paper mill
   d) The Narrows
   e) a ferry crossing
   f) a spit
   g) the braided course of a river
   h) a sea loch or fjord.

Look at the map of Ingleton on page 58 and at the aerial photograph opposite on page 59.

7. Find the approximate position of the camera when the photograph was taken. *Clue:* Line up the streets linking the houses in the bottom right-hand quarter of the photograph.
8. Locate the following features on both the map and the photograph:
   a) a viaduct
   b) a school
   c) a quarry
   d) the approximate position of a waterfall
   e) a caravan site
   f) Twistleton Scar End.
9. Describe and use evidence on the map to explain the distribution of woodland on the photograph.

Look at the map of the Bernese Oberland on page 64 and at the photograph on page 74.

10. Find the approximate position of the camera when the photograph was taken from a position close to the Eigergletscher Station on the mountain railway. In which direction was the camera pointing?
11. What is the name of the mountain on the left? How high is the peak in the middle? What is the name of the physical feature on the right? Identify the following features on the photograph and on the map:
    a) the snout of a glacier
    b) an arête
    c) a corrie or cirque
    d) a terminal or lateral moraine
    e) crevasses.

Compare the two aerial photographs on pages 62 and 63.

12. What are the advantages and the disadvantages of:
    a) a vertical aerial photograph?
    b) an oblique aerial photograph?
13. Find a map of central London in a road book or atlas. Work out the scale of the vertical aerial photograph.
14. Draw a linear scale for use with the vertical aerial photograph.
15. Can you use the vertical aerial photograph in the same way as a map?
16. Use the oblique aerial photograph to identify these London landmarks on the vertical aerial photograph:
    a) Tower Bridge
    b) London Bridge
    c) London Bridge railway station
    d) HMS Belfast
    e) the Tower of London
    f) St Paul's Cathedral
    g) St James's Park
    h) St Katharine's Docks.
17. Use the vertical aerial photograph to identify the approximate camera position and angle of view used to take the oblique aerial photograph.
18. Use a street map of central London to identify the following features on the vertical aerial photograph:
    a) Waterloo Station
    b) Liverpool Street Station
    c) The Aldwych and the Strand
    d) Houses of Parliament
    e) Trafalgar Square.

Oblique aerial photograph of the River Thames and central London

Vertical aerial photograph of central London

Contour maps

Relief is shown in three main ways on Ordnance Survey maps:

- by metric contour lines. These are lines (such as the 50-metre contour line) which join up places which are all the same height above sea level;

- by a black dot indicating the position on the map where the height of the ground above sea level has been accurately surveyed. This is called a *spot height* (e.g. ·251 – meaning 251 metres above sea level);

- by a dot in a triangle also indicating the position on the map where the height of the ground above sea level has been accurately surveyed. This is called a *triangulation point* (e.g. △ 120 – meaning 120 metres above sea level).

Sometimes, on maps printed in atlases for example, only a small number of contours are used to pick out the upland and lowland areas and the regions of high mountains. Different colours or different types of shading indicate land at different heights (e.g. 0–200 metres, 200–500 metres, 500–1000 metres, and so on).

Contour maps help us to picture the shape of the land (how it rises and falls) and to identify different physical features or landforms. You can recognise many of these landforms from their distinctive contour shapes (see pages 93–4).

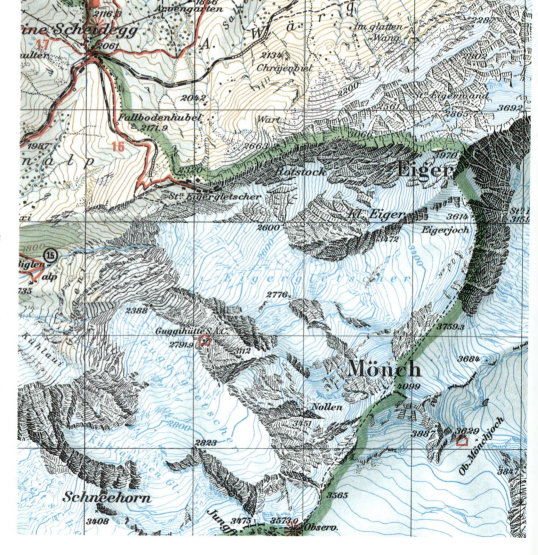

Study carefully this Swiss map of part of the Bernese Oberland in the Alps. It has been drawn to a scale of 1:33 333 and shows the Eiger, one of the most famous mountains in the world, and also the Eigergletscher (Eiger Glacier).

How have the Swiss cartographers (the people who draw maps) shown the relief of the land – its height above sea level and its appearance? Compare their methods with those used by the British cartographers working for the Ordnance Survey who drew the map of Fort William on page 56

Contour maps 65

How to find heights by reading the contours

On the Map	Height	Clue
(triangulation point ▲76)	76 m	Triangulation point
(● dot)	60 m	Although the 60 m contour is not numbered count the contours at 10 m intervals from the 40 m contour line
(♦ on 40 m contour)	40 m	40 m contour
(■)	35 m	35 m because it is halfway between the 30 m and 40 m contours
(■)	28 m	28 m because it is halfway between spot height 26 m and the 30 m contour
(26 •)	26 m	26 m spot height
(∗)	22 m	22 m because it is two tenths of the distance from the 20 m contour to the 30 m contour

EXERCISES

Look at the Ordnance Survey map of Fort William on page 56.

1. Give the grid reference of:
   a) a triangulation point
   b) a spot height.

2. Place tracing paper over the map and draw in the 500 metre and 1000 metre contours. Colour or shade your tracing so that it shows land:
   a) below 500 metres
   b) between 500 and 1000 metres
   c) land over 1000 metres.

Look at the Ordnance Survey map of Ingleton on page 58.

3. Draw a map to show the relief of this area. Choose two or three contour lines to separate the different areas and trace the appropriate contour lines using fine tracing paper.

Look at the Swiss relief map on page 64.

4. What metric contour interval has been used on this map? What other methods of showing relief have been used? What do you think is the significance of the use of blue to show some of the contour lines?

5. Draw a sketch map to show the relief of this area, using different colours to show the glaciers and the bare rock faces on the mountain sides.

Drawing a cross-section

A good way of picturing the rise and fall of the land is to draw a cross-section *exactly* to scale or to draw a sketch section *approximately* to scale (see page 68).
 A cross-section is simply a graph which uses the contour lines as data to give a pictorial impression of the rise and fall of the ground.

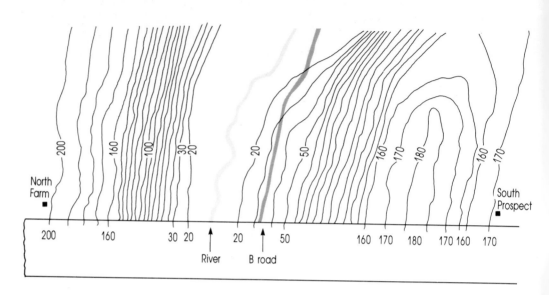

1 Locate on the map the two points between which your cross-section will be drawn.

2 Place a long straight edge of paper between these points and mark and number all the contours between them where they cross the line. Where the contours are close together and evenly spaced it is unnecessary to mark anything other than the lowest and highest contours.

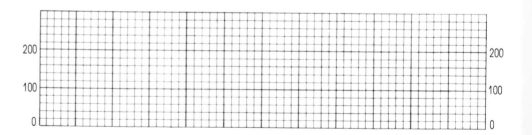

3 Draw your cross-section on graph paper divided into 2 mm squares Each interval of 2 mm will be used to represent a fixed difference in height.

4 Place the marked straight edge of paper on the graph. Draw in the base line of the cross-section at the bottom of the graph paper. This line represents sea-level, so label it 0 metres on the vertical scale.

5 The horizontal scale will be the same as that of the map but the vertical scale will have to be chosen carefully so that it exaggerates the relief of the land by about five times. Otherwise hills which you may think steep will appear to be very gentle undulations when drawn exactly to scale.

In general, if the highest point on the cross-section is no more than 500 metres then make each vertical square on your grid represent a height of *10 metres* on the 1:25 000 map series or *20 metres* on the 1:50 000 map series.

If the highest point to be shown on the cross-section is over 500 metres make each 2 mm square represent *25 metres* on the 1:25 000 map series or *50 metres* on the 1:50 000 map series.

6 Label the vertical intervals on the grid of your cross-section. Place the annotated straight edge of paper on this grid and use a sharp pencil to mark off each contour on its matching grid line.

7 Join the points together to make a fine even outline.

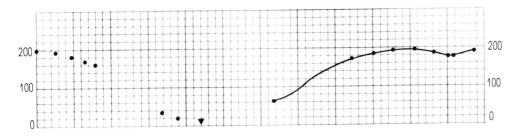

8 If you have been asked to insert other detail on the section (such as the position of a river or town) mark this on the outline as well. With practice you will mark these details on the straight edge of paper as you annotate the contours.

9 Add the finishing touches. Ensure that the horizontal and vertical scales are correctly shown on the cross-section. Mark in the grid references for the two terminal points on the cross-section. Give your cross-section a title.

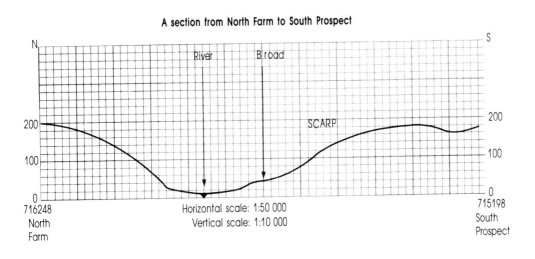

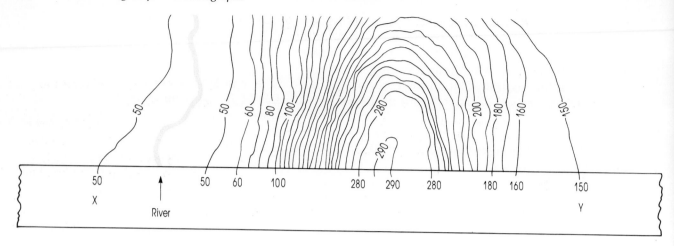

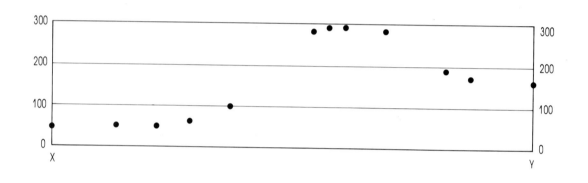

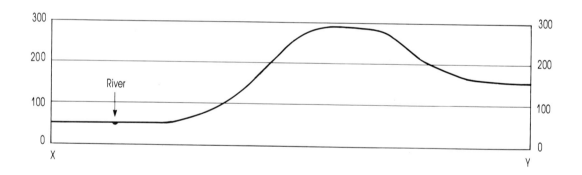

Drawing a sketch section

You may sometimes be asked to draw a sketch section between two points. Follow the same procedure as for a cross-section *but* mark off and number only the significant contours, such as the top and bottom of a hill.

With practice you should be able to draw a sketch section like this freehand, without marking off the contours first of all on a straight edge of paper. The purpose of the sketch section is to gain a rough idea of the rise and fall of the land, not a precise graph plotting in every contour.

EXERCISES

Look at the map of Ingleton on page 58.

1 Draw a cross-section between the spot height 430 metres in grid square 7274 and Glebe Farm (grid reference 688742). Mark in and name Glebe Farm, Twistleton Manor House, the River Wiss, a quarry, and a main road.

Look at the map of Fort William on page 56.

2 Draw a sketch section to show the rise and fall of the ground between Stronchreggan in grid square 0772 and Ben Nevis in grid square 1671.

Gradients and slopes

Words like 'steep' and 'very steep' are often used to describe slopes. Although these are useful descriptive words, it is possible to be more precise. This is because the average angle of a slope can be calculated exactly after close examination of the contours. Gradients are often expressed as ratios, such as 1:7 or 1 in 7. This simply means that a slope rises one metre in height for every seven metres forward. If you climb a 1 in 5 hill, you climb one metre in height for every five metres forward (or one foot in height for every five feet forward).

On Ordnance Survey maps the gradients on many roads are shown by symbols, with one arrow indicating a gradient between 1 in 5 and 1 in 7, and two arrows indicating a gradient steeper than 1 in 5. You can calculate the gradient between two points on a map if you follow this method:

1 Measure the distance between the two points *in metres*.

2 Find the difference in height *in metres* between the two points. If you have any difficulty use the chart on page 65 to help you work out the heights from spot heights or contours.

3 Divide the distance between the two points by the difference in height to find the gradient. For example, if the height of point A is 30 metres above sea level and point B is on the 50-metre contour line then the difference in *height* (or altitude) between the two places is 20 metres. If the distance on the ground between them is 280 metres, we can calculate the *gradient* by dividing the distance (280 metres) by the difference in height (20 metres), that is 280 ÷ 20 = 14. So the gradient is 1 in 14 or 1:14.

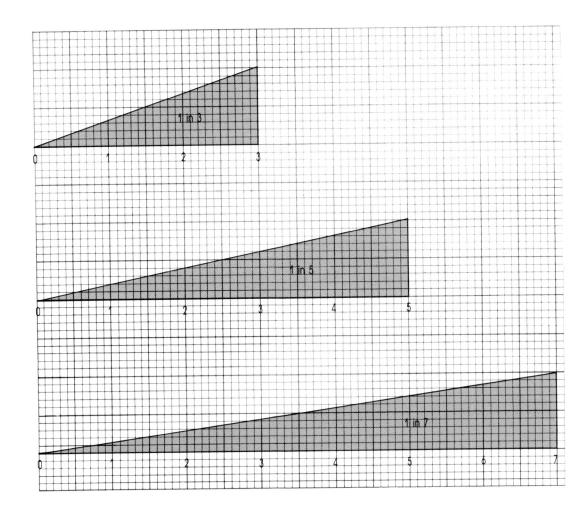

EXERCISES

1. What is the gradient on a stretch of road 500 metres long, which rises 25 metres from a point 130 metres above sea level to one which is 155 metres in height?

2. What would the gradient be if the difference in height between the points on the 500-metre stretch of road was 83 metres?

Look at the Ordnance Survey map of Fort William on page 56.

3. What is the average gradient on the mountain path between the point near the bridge across the stream (Allt a Mhuilinn) at grid reference 140756 and the Mountain Rescue Post at 167722.

4. What gradient would you have to ascend if you climbed in a straight line from the camp site in Glen Nevis (124723) to the summit of Meall an t-Suidhe (139729)?

Estimating area on a map

You can estimate the area of a feature on a map, diagram or graph by the counting squares method.

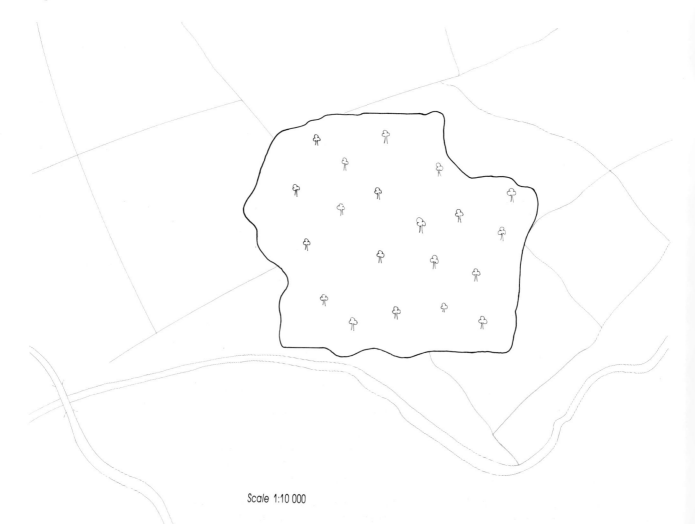

Scale 1:10 000

Estimating area on a map

1. Trace an outline of the area to be measured, such as a lake or woodland area.

2. Place the traced outline on top of graph paper already divided into 2 mm squares.

3. Count the total number of squares completely enclosed by the traced outline. Use shortcuts, like those shown on the diagram, to count large blocks of 100 or 25 squares.

4. Where the traced outline goes partly through a square count it as either a quarter, half, or three-quarter square. Use a tally sheet (see page 24) to count these part-squares as in Table 1.

5. Check the scale of the map you are using.

6. Multiply the total number of squares by the appropriate factor in Table 2 to give the area of the feature in either square metres, hectares, or square kilometres.

7. In the example the total number of squares is

   6 × 100 = 600
   6 × 25 = 150
   Remainder = 210
   Total = 960 squares

   On the 1:10 000 scale multiply the total (960) by a factor of 0.04 to give the area of the woodland in hectares:
   960 × 0.04 = 38.4 hectares.

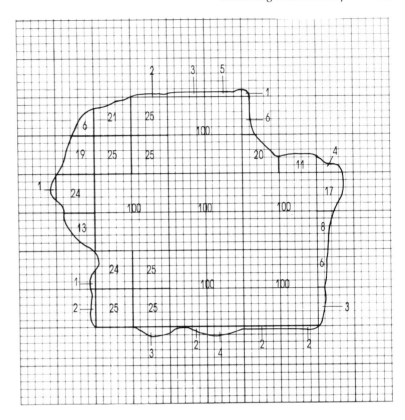

Table 1

Quarter squares	Half squares	Three-quarter squares
ℋℋ ℋℋ I	ℋℋ III	ℋℋ II
11 × 0.25 squares	8 × 0.5 squares	7 × 0.75 squares
= 2.75 squares	= 4.0 squares	= 5.25 squares
Total = 2.75 + 4.0 + 5.25 = 12 squares		

Table 2

Map scale	If you want the answer in		
	square metres	hectares	square kilometres
	Multiply by	Multiply by	Multiply by
1:50 000	10 000	1	0.01
1:25 000	2500	0.25	0.0025
1:10 000	400	0.04	0.0004
1:2500	25	0.0025	0.000 025
1:1250	6.25	0.000 625	0.000 006 25

EXERCISES

Look at the Ordnance Survey map on page 56.

1. What is the area of the woodland near Corpach Hill (grid squares 0877, 0878, 0977, 0978?

2. What is the total area of sea on this map?

3. Find the 1000-metre contour line. Trace the boundary of the area on the map which is over 1000 metres in height. Calculate its area in hectacres.

4. What percentage of the total land area shown on the map is over 1000 metres in height?

Look at the map of Ingleton on page 58.

5. Calculate the area covered by the map.

6. Estimate (as accurately as you can) the total area of land covered with limestone pavement and bare rocks (e.g. White Scars at grid reference 7274).

7. What percentage of the Ingleton area is covered by bare rock and limestone pavement?

Patterns on a map

In geography we often study maps to see if we can see a pattern. We look to see if there is a link between the distribution of settlements on the map, such as towns, villages, and farms, and the physical geography of the area. How are the settlements related to the spread of high land, to the drainage pattern, to the coast, rocks, or soils? Is there an important link between the distribution of settlements and other aspects of the human geography of the area, such as the road system, the distribution of industry, or the growth of a tourist industry?

Distribution maps can be divided into three main types according to the way in which they plot data:

- maps using lines, such as contour lines, to join places which have the same thing in common, are called *isopleth* (or sometimes *isoline*) maps;
- maps using colours or shading to show patches on the map are called *choropleth* maps;
- maps using points, such as dots or symbols, are called *dot distribution* maps (such as a map showing the position of farmhouses in a rural area or a map of population).

Distribution maps like these can be made from Ordnance Survey maps by making *selective tracings*.

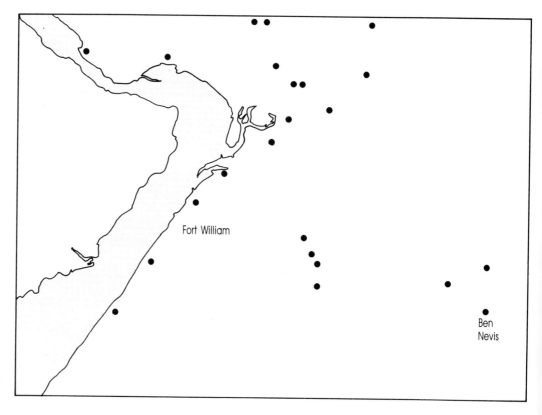

Dot distribution map showing features related to the tourist and mountain climbing attractions of the area close to Fort William (see map on page 56)

EXERCISES

1 Where are these tourist features situated? Are they situated on the highland or on the lowland? Are they in the country or in the town? Are they close to the coast, on a river, or close to a road or railway or canal?

2 Draw a dot distribution map of the features related to the tourist industry to be found on the map of Ingleton on page 58.

MAKING A SELECTIVE TRACING

1. Place a sheet of fine tracing paper over the map.

2. Mark in certain key reference points so that you can always place the tracing paper exactly over the area of the map you are studying (in case you are interrupted as you work).

3. Then plot with dots, symbols, or colours, the distribution of the feature you have selected for study, such as:
    water features (streams, rivers, lakes, ponds)
    land use features (such as woodland, orchards)
    farming features (such as the position of all the farms on the map)
    settlement features (such as the position of all farmhouses, villages and towns)
    transport features (such as the position of all the railways and roads on the map).

4. See if you can relate the distribution pattern on your map to a similar distribution of some other feature, such as a map of woodland compared with one of the drainage system.

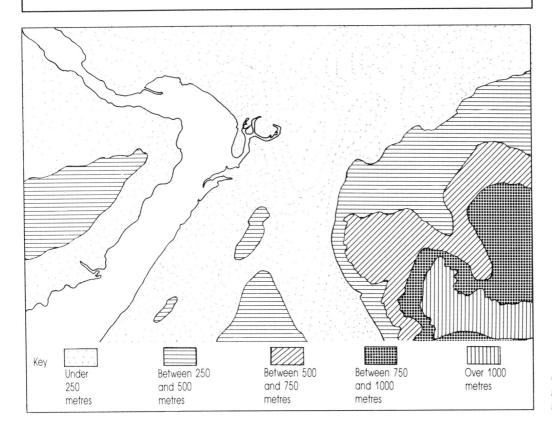

Choropleth map showing the relief of the Fort William area

EXERCISE

Find out about the area served by your nearest large town or city. Obtain a copy of one of the local newspapers printed in the town, preferably one with plenty of advertisements. Trace an outline map of the town and its surrounding area. Mark with a dot the approximate position of every garage advertising cars for sale. Use a different coloured dot to mark the position of every house for sale. Use yet another coloured dot to mark the position of all towns and villages mentioned in local news items. Study the completed map and see if you can see any pattern in the distribution of the three types of coloured dot.

Map interpretation

Map reading is when you identify points, patches, and lines on a map; when you draw cross-sections or make selective traces; or when you find the gradient between two points.

Map interpretation is when you deduce things from a map (such as reasons for the growth of an industry), when you see patterns and relationships (such as the distribution of prehistoric remains on upland rather than lowland sites), and when you find out things from a map which have not been put there deliberately by the map makers (such as the clues which tell you about the growth and development of a large town). Sometimes you can see an effect and suggest a possible cause from map evidence on its own.

Finding reasons for the distributions and patterns you see on a map can be assisted by many of the map reading exercises mentioned earlier, such as drawing a cross-section or making a selective tracing to pick out specific distributions (the drainage pattern, uplands, settlements, or woodland, for example). There is a list of these map reading techniques opposite.

Close examination of a map in a chalkland area, for example, might reveal the location of a string of villages at the foot of an escarpment, all at approximately the same height above sea level, and all at a point where springs issue from the chalk. We call these *spring-line settlements*. In seeing a relationship like this between relief, underlying rocks, drainage, and settlement patterns we interpret the evidence provided by the map. It is one thing (map reading) to identify a spring or settlement on a map, but quite another thing (map interpretation) to use the same information to find out something of significance about the geography of the area shown on the map.

In the reference section (pages 86–127) you will find clues which will help you to interpret Ordnance Survey maps. But do bear in mind that every map is different. No two areas are the same. Every map or map extract you see is unique. Do not expect to see identical features on the maps you study. You will have to use your skills in map reading, *and* your intelligence, to work out what a map can tell you about an area.

The best way to look upon map interpretation is as a puzzle or detective mystery. The answers are staring you in the face if only you can solve the clues!

Look at the map of Switzerland on page 64. This photograph was taken from the Eigergletscher (Eiger Glacier) Station on the mountain railway. What extra information does the map give you about this area which you cannot deduce from the photograph?

MAP READING TECHNIQUES FOR MAP INTERPRETATION

- Draw *sketch sections* to get an idea of the rise and fall of the land.
- Identify the main *compass directions* to determine the direction in which any prominent slopes on the map are facing (north-facing slopes get little sun, south-facing slopes get most sun). Are the villages and towns on the map south-facing? Do the corries in a glaciated area face north?
- Relate the evidence shown on the map to evidence shown on any aerial or ground-level photographs you have of the area.
- What evidence is there of the ways in which local people get a living from the land? Is there any evidence of farming? Do the place names or farm names tell you anything about the type of farming? What types of land use are depicted on the map? What evidence is there of industry, such as a cement works, a mine, a power station, an unnamed industrial complex or an iron and steel works?
- What do the other symbols on the map reveal about the area, such as power lines and orchards?
- What do the transport symbols tell you about the area? Are there any motorways or dual carriageways? Are there any railway services? Are there any ports and airports?
- How far apart are the villages and towns? What is their relationship to one another? How can you tell that some towns provide services which the others do not provide?
- Is there any evidence of a tourist industry? Are there any hotels marked on the map? Are there any seaside piers, National Trust properties, etc?
- Is there any evidence to tell you about the growth of the largest town on the map?
- Can you identify any spring-line settlements, towns situated at crossing points on a river or estuary, towns or villages on a dry site above damp land, towns or villages which would have been in a good defensive position in the past, towns or villages on the lowest bridging point across a river?

EXERCISES

Look at the maps on pages 56 and 58.

1 Quote map evidence to suggest reasons why Fort William and Ingleton are important tourist centres.

2 What clues are there to the types of farming to be seen in the areas covered by these maps?

USING STATISTICS

Statistics

If you make a land-use survey of a farm, you may be tempted to write that 'the farmer grows a lot of barley' or that 'only a small amount of the land is sown with turnips'. In geography, however, we prefer to use exact numbers (*statistics*) to say how much, how many, how long, or how heavy.

You will get more credit if you can say, for instance, that the results of your land-use survey show that last year 79 out of the 160 hectares on the farm were sown with barley and only 14 with turnips.

Note that these farm statistics are related to a specific period ('last year'). Fields sown with crops change from year to year. This is why statistics of production are meaningless unless accompanied by dates indicating clearly the period for which the statistics were counted.

You should be beware, however, of the very great temptation to treat numbers as ends in themselves. Statistics can often help to prove or disprove an assertion but they can also be subject to error. It depends partly on how accurately they have been collected and whether they really can measure something exactly to everyone's satisfaction. To do this they must be independent of the person collecting the statistics. In other words, the totals will always be the same no matter who counts or measures them. This is not always the case. For instance, suppose you count commercial vehicles on one side of the road and one of your friends counts the same vehicles on the other side. You may have decided to class heavy goods vehicles (such as lorries) as one category and light goods vehicles (such as vans) as another. It seems clearcut but it is not. Some of the vehicles you see on the road might be classed as light goods vehicles by some people and as heavy goods vehicles by others.

Printed statistics will be your main source for many of the statistics you use in your studies. Most libraries have up-to-date editions of standard reference works (encyclopaedias, gazetteers, and almanacs) which contain statistics of population growth, weather records, production figures for crops and products, and other relevant records. If you need data of this kind you may well be able to find what you are looking for in:

- *Whitaker's Almanack* (especially for the UK);
- *The Statesman's Year Book* (statistics for every country in the world);
- *The World Almanac* (especially for the USA and Canada);
- *Philip's Pocket Guide to the World* (especially for weather records and production statistics);
- *Quid,* if you can read French (especially for Europe).

You can also find statistics you may be able to use in:

- railway, airport, and bus timetables;
- official census reports for the United Kingdom;
- *European Historical Statistics 1750–1975* (for statistics of population, industrial and agricultural production, transport, employment, etc.);
- newspapers and magazines; and many other published sources as well.

The significance of raw statistics on their own is often hard to grasp. This is why statistics are often converted into graphs, percentages, and averages to make them easier to understand. We can then see if they reveal patterns or relationships which provide us with useful geographical information.

- Plotting statistics on a *graph* (see below) is a very good way of seeking a pattern in a set of numbers which otherwise look rather meaningless in a table.

- You can use statistics to work out *averages* (see page 81), such as mean annual rainfall, average number of hours of sunshine in July, mean milk production on a farm in January, or the average size and shape of pebbles on a beach. Averages help to say what is typical of a district, country or region, such as the average life expectancy of an infant or the average size of a farm in hectares.

- You can often make more sense of raw statistics if you use them to work out *percentages,* such as the percentage of farmland on the 160 hectare farm under barley (49 per cent) or under turnips (9 per cent). You can see on page 82 how to deal with percentages relating to small samples and how they can be used to forecast overall percentages.

- You can also use statistics to work out how closely two sets of figures are related to one another. *Scatter graphs* and *rank correlations* (see page 83–5) help you to search for patterns in the statistics you have collected, such as a comparison between infant mortality figures and those for literacy (ability to read and write).

Graphs

Statistics in themselves are meaningless. They only make sense if we can see a pattern or a trend in the statistics. This is why we often plot them on a map or on a graph. It is easier to see a pattern this way.

You can see how statistics have been used to draw the different types of graph shown on these pages. What patterns do they reveal?

A line graph

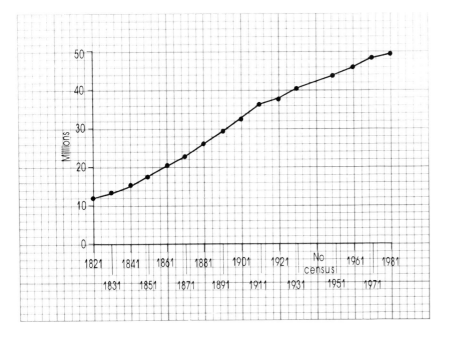

Population of England and Wales 1821–1981 (millions)	
1821	12.0
1831	13.9
1841	15.9
1851	17.9
1861	20.1
1871	22.7
1881	26.0
1891	29.0
1901	32.5
1911	36.1
1921	37.6
1931	40.0
1951	43.8
1961	46.1
1971	48.8
1981	49.2

NB No census in 1941

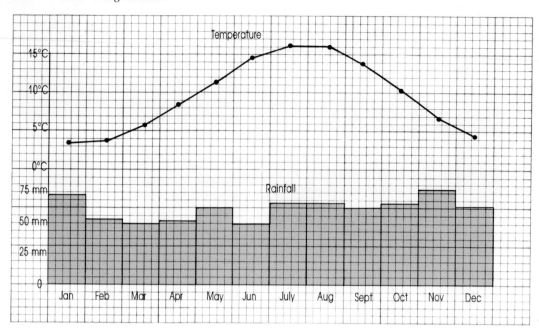

A climograph

Average annual rainfall and mean monthly temperatures in Birmingham

	Jan	Feb	Mar	Apr	May	June	July	Aug	Sept	Oct	Nov	Dec
Mean monthly temperature (°C)	3.5	3.7	5.9	8.5	11.5	14.6	16.3	16.1	13.7	10.1	6.7	4.7
Rainfall (mm)	74	54	50	53	64	50	69	69	61	69	84	67

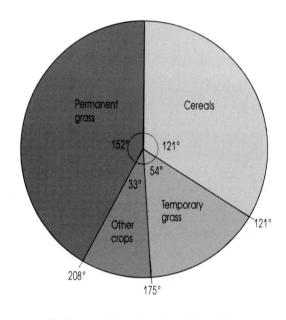

A pie chart

Cultivated land in the UK, 1984

Type of cultivation	Hectares (000s)	Angle*	Cumulative angle
Cereals	4037	121°	121°
Temporary grass	1794	54°	175°
Other crops	1117	33°	208°
Permanent grass	5105	152°	360°
TOTAL	12 053	360°	

$$\text{*Angle} = \frac{\text{area in hectares}}{\text{total area (12 053)}} \times 360$$

A bar graph

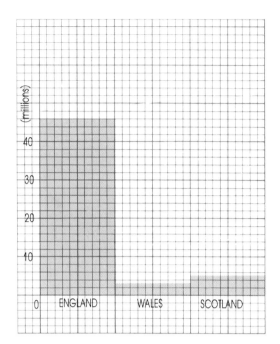

Population of Great Britain 1981 (millions)	
England	46.4
Wales	2.8
Scotland	5.1

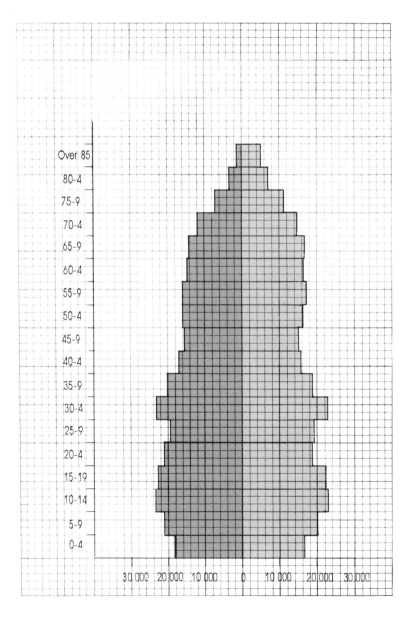

An age–sex pyramid

The age and sex distribution for the county of Suffolk, 1981

Age last birthday	No. of males (000s)	No. of females (000s)
0–4	18.8	17.9
5–9	20.9	20.0
10–14	23.8	22.7
15–19	23.6	22.2
20–4	21.0	18.9
25–9	19.3	19.2
30–4	23.2	22.8
35–9	20.0	19.1
40–4	17.1	16.1
45–9	15.8	15.3
50–4	16.0	16.1
55–9	16.0	17.0
60–4	14.7	16.6
65–9	14.6	16.9
70–4	12.0	15.3
75–9	7.9	11.5
80–4	3.6	7.1
85+	1.9	5.3

Source: 1981 census

A *histogram* is a special type of bar graph which shows the distribution of occurrences of each value, or group of values on either side of the average or mean. In a histogram, the area of each bar is proportional to the class frequency. As you can see from the histogram opposite, if these occurrences are plotted on a bar graph they normally produce a symmetrical pattern, with the highest bar in the middle and the other bars tapering off gradually on either side.

If the same data are plotted on a line graph they will usually produce a similar pattern, called the *normal probability curve*. The bar graph and normal probability curve here were drawn from the following statistics:

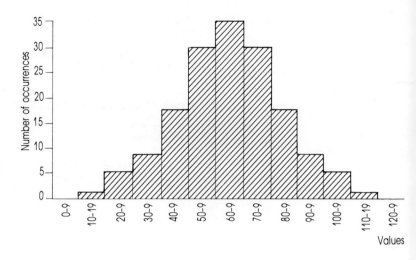

0–9	0
10–19	1
20–9	5
30–9	9
40–9	17
50–9	30
60–9	35
70–9	30
80–9	17
90–9	9
100–9	5
110–19	1
120–9	0

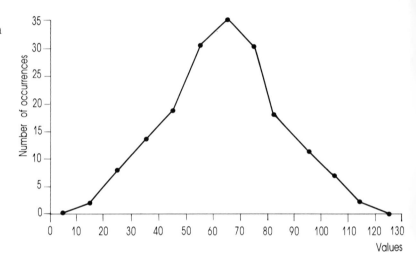

EXERCISES

1 Draw a histogram and a normal probability curve for the following atmospheric pressure readings taken over the course of a year at a weather station:

Atmospheric pressure	Number of days
980 mb to 983 mb	1
984 mb to 987 mb	3
988 mb to 991 mb	6
992 mb to 995 mb	27
996 mb to 999 mb	25
1000 mb to 1003 mb	49
1004 mb to 1007 mb	59
1008 mb to 1011 mb	51
1012 mb to 1015 mb	52
1016 mb to 1019 mb	41
1020 mb to 1023 mb	23
1024 mb to 1027 mb	15
1028 mb to 1031 mb	5
1032 mb to 1035 mb	5
1036 mb to 1039 mb	2
1040 mb to 1043 mb	1

2 What deductions can you make about atmospheric pressure at that weather station from your histogram and graph?

3 What information can you deduce from the age–sex pyramid on page 79? On average who live longer, men or women? Are the chances of a boy or girl baby being born equal?

4 What are the advantages and disadvantages of a pie chart compared with a bar graph? Which of the graphs on pages 77–9 would you choose to show how coal production has declined in Britain in the last 50 years? How would you show the different outputs by value on a farm:
a) if you already knew the total value of those outputs;
b) if you only knew some of those outputs?

How would you show the variation in pebble size on the bed of a river?

5 Write a description of population growth in England and Wales since 1821 using information you can deduce from the line graph on page 77.

6 What patterns can you find in the climograph of Birmingham on page 78?

7 Draw a pie chart to show the data in the table opposite.

8 Suggest an explanation for the high proportion of people born in North America living in an English county.

People living in Suffolk but born outside the British Isles (by continents), 1981

Asia (including Turkey and USSR)	4693
Australasia	913
Central and South America	1931
Africa	1818
Europe	6672
North America	19 758
Rest of world (including islands)	148

Averages

People often talk about the average height or weight of a person. Almost always they have in mind the *arithmetic mean* rather than any of the other averages which can also be calculated from a given set of values:

> The arithmetic mean is calculated by adding up the values and dividing the sum by the number of values.
> Thus 4 + 12 + 12 + 16 + 17 + 12 + 4 = 77
> So the arithmetic mean is 77 ÷ 7 (the number of values) = 11

As you can see only two of the numbers in the sample are actually under 11. The other five numbers are all higher than the arithmetic mean of 11. In circumstances like this you might choose to calculate the *median* as the average instead. The median often gives a better idea of what is typical. It can be calculated easily without a calculator, since it is simply the middle-ranking number in any set of numbers:

> Put the numbers in rank order (meaning in order of size) and find the value of the number in the middle.
> Thus in the sequence: 17, 16, 12, *12*, 12, 4, 4, the middle ranking number is obviously 12, since there are an equal number of numbers above and below it. If two numbers tied for the median position we would add them together and then find their arithmetic mean.

Sometimes we prefer to calculate yet another type of average. This is called the *mode*:

> It is found by simply working out which is the most commonly occurring number in a set of numbers (for example the value of the tallest bar in a histogram or the peak of the normal probability curve).
> In the sequence of numbers above the mode is also 12, since this is the value of three of the seven numbers.

EXERCISES

1 What is the average size of field in the sample of fields on the south-facing slopes of the North York Moors below? Work out the arithmetic mean, the median, and the mode.

			Area in hectares			
0.8	3.5	7.1	3.8	7.9	1.2	1.8
4.1	2.0	4.3	6.4	3.1	3.0	4.8
2.7	4.8	4.5	2.7	3.2	5.6	

2 See if you can work out the arithmetic mean, median, and mode of the atmospheric pressure readings on page 80.

Sampling and percentages

Some statistics, such as opinion polls, are obviously only a sample of all the possible statistics which could have been taken at the same time. For instance, if you ask 100 shoppers to complete a questionnaire and you find that 33 shop at a supermarket only once a week you cannot be certain that the same percentage will also apply to the hundreds of other shoppers in the precinct or shopping centre at the same time. Your sample of 33 per cent is subject to *sampling error*. This is why statisticians have worked out a way of testing to see what the true percentage is likely to be on the basis of your sample. They do this by calculating the margin of error which you would have to allow on either side of the sample percentage to be fairly safe in predicting what the true percentage would be if you could count everything instead of just a small sample.

Suppose we pick out 59 yellow counters and 41 blue counters from a huge box containing thousands of blue and yellow counters. What is the true percentage of yellow counters in the box? How close is it to 59 per cent?

METHOD FOR TESTING A SAMPLE PERCENTAGE

1	Note down the total number of samples taken and call this number N.	Since there are 100 counters in the sample $N = 100$
2	Work out the sample percentage and call it $p\%$	The sample percentage of yellow counters is $59\% = p\%$
3	Subtract $p\%$ from 100% and call the result $q\%$	$100\% - 59\% = 41\% = q\%$
4	Multiply $p\%$ by $q\%$	$p\% \times q\% = 59 \times 41 = 2419$
5	Divide by N	$\dfrac{2419}{N} = \dfrac{2419}{100} = 24.19$
6	Find the square root of this number = the *margin of error*.	$\sqrt{24.19} = 4.918 = 4.9$
7	Work out the range within which the true percentage $P\%$ will lie from the sample percentage $p\%$ plus (+) or minus (−) *twice* the margin of error	Twice the margin of error of $4.9 = 9.8\%$. So the true percentage of yellow counters in the box probably lies somewhere between: $59 - 9.8\% = 49.2\%$ and $59 + 9.8\% = 68.8\%$

EXERCISES

1 Assume that you have sampled 1000 counters instead of 100 and you still find that 59 per cent are yellow. Work out whether the true percentage of yellow counters still lies between 49.2 per cent and 68.8 per cent.

2 What important lesson can you learn from the answer to Exercise 1?

3 A local newspaper opinion poll tells you that 53.2 per cent of people questioned, out of a sample of 731 people, say they intend to vote for Labour at a local election (with only two candidates). Only 46.8 per cent say they will vote for the Conservative candidate. Are the Labour Party councillors safe to assume their candidate will be elected?

Making comparisons

In geography we often need to compare two sets of data to see if there is any link between the two. We may discover that the more there is of one thing (such as height above sea level), the more there is of the other as well (such as rainfall). When two sets of data tend to agree in this way we say they are *positively correlated*.

Sometimes we discover that two sets of data tend to disagree. The more there is of one thing (such as distance from a sugar-beet factory), the less there is of the other (such as production of sugar beet). When two sets of data tend to disagree like this we say they are *negatively correlated*.

Often there is no obvious or direct link between two sets of data.

Even if there is a positive or negative correlation the statistics in themselves *are not enough to prove that the one causes the other*. Instead, they may each be related to a third group of statistics.

It is possible, for example, to collect statistics to show that the importance of tourism (such as the number of hotel beds) in towns in the Lake District increases with rainfall. The wetter the place, the greater the number of tourists!

Now we know that holidaymakers do not ordinarily seek out wet places for holidays. So how do we account for this fact? The answer is quite simple:

a) The tourists are attracted by the mountains.
b) Rainfall in Britain almost always increases with height.

In other words, both sets of data – numbers of tourists and rainfall statistics – are each related to a third set of statistics – height above sea level.

You can use either of the following methods to study the extent to which two sets of data match each other by:

- calculating the *rank correlation coefficient;*
- drawing a *scatter graph.*

Calculating the rank correlation coefficient

We can measure how closely two sets of data agree with one another if we work out the degree of *correlation* between them. This varies between +1.0 (the highest positive correlation possible) and −1.0 (the highest negative correlation possible). A correlation coefficient of 0, halfway between the two, simply means that no relationship has yet been proved, either way, between the two sets of data.

A correlation coefficient of +0.8 or +0.9 usually means a high degree of *positive correlation*. It tells you that the two sets of figures are closely related – the more of one, the more of the other. A correlation of −0.8 or −0.9, on the other hand, usually means a high degree of *negative correlation* – the more of one, the less of the other.

A correlation coefficient of +0.3, +0.2, +0.1, −0.1, −0.2, −0.3 usually means that there is little relationship between the two sets of data.

Method

Suppose you have two sets of statistics for a number of places such as villages, towns, farms, factories, countries, etc. (In the example on these pages the statistics are for annual rainfall and height above sea-level.)

1. Draw up a table like the one on page 84.

2. Sort the first set of statistics (e.g. Rain) in order of size. This is called *rank order*. First place (rank 1) goes to the highest number. Second place goes to the second highest number (rank 2), and so on.

3. If two or more places share the same number, add together the ranks they all share and divide it by the number of places sharing the same rank.

   Thus if four places all come fifth they share ranks 5, 6, 7 and 8. Add 5 + 6 + 7 + 8 = 26. Divide 26 by the number of places, 26 ÷ 4 = 6.5. So all four places are given the rank of 6.5. Do not forget, however, that the next rank after these four places is 9.

			Columns			
1	2	3	4	5	6	7
Place	Rain (mm)	Height (metres)	Rain rank	Height rank	D	D^2
A	1270	275	1	1	0	0
B	1210	230	2	2	0	0
C	1075	90	3.5	4.5	1	1
D	1075	50	3.5	6	2.5	6.25
E	1065	100	5	3	2	4
F	1025	90	6	4.5	1.5	2.25
G	980	40	7	7	0	0
H	900	20	8	8	0	0
$N = 8$						$\Sigma D^2 = 13.5$

4 List the places in column 1 by order of these ranks (e.g. Rain). List the statistics in column 2 and show the rank order of these statistics 1, 2, 3, 4, 5, etc., in column 4.

5 List the statistics for the second set of data (e.g. Height) in column 3.

6 Work out the order of ranks for this second set of statistics (e.g. Height) and list the ranks 1, 2, 3, 4, 5, etc., in column 5.

7 Subtract the rank in column 4 from the rank in column 5 or vice versa (whichever is the smaller number). Call this value D (for the difference) and put it in column 6.

8 Square the number D in column 6. Put it in column 7 (D^2).

9 Add up the values of D^2 in column 7. The sum of these values is ΣD^2. As you can see this is 13.5 in the example.

10 Add up the number of places in column 1 (this is called N). As you can see this is 8 in the example.

11 Insert the values for ΣD^2 and N in the formula:

$$1 - \frac{6 \times \Sigma D^2}{(N \times N \times N) - N}$$

By calculation this becomes:

$$1 - \frac{6 \times 13.5}{(8 \times 8 \times 8) - 8} = 1 - \frac{81}{512 - 8}$$

$$= 1 - \frac{81}{504}$$

$$= 1 - 0.16$$

$$= +0.84$$

So the extent to which the two sets of statistics are related – annual rainfall and height above sea-level – has been measured by the rank correlation coefficient as being +0.84. The + tells us that it is a positive correlation, the higher you are above sea-level, the greater the rainfall. The index of +0.84 tells us that the degree of correlation is high, since the maximum possible is +1.0.

Drawing a scatter graph

Another way of showing the same data is to draw a scatter graph like the one below. As you can see the figure for height above sea-level (in metres) for each weather station has been plotted against its annual rainfall (in millimetres). What can you deduce from this scatter graph?

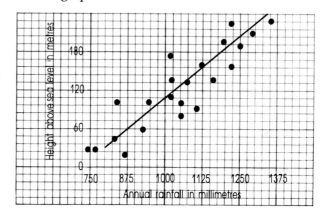

As you can see, there is a distinctive pattern. This has been highlighted by the *trend line* which has been drawn in between the dots.

Most scatter graphs produce one of four main types of pattern – *positive, negative, random,* or *clustered.* These are illustrated below.

A positive pattern in a scatter graph is indicated by a trend line from the bottom left-hand corner to the top right. It shows that there is a positive correlation between the two sets of data. The higher the value of one, the higher the value of the other.

A negative (or inverse) pattern in a scatter graph is indicated by a trend line from the top left-hand corner to the bottom right. It shows that there is a negative correlation between the two sets of data. The higher the value of one, the lower the value of the other.

A random pattern in a scatter graph is indicated when there is no recognisable pattern (that you can see) in the distribution of the dots in the graph.

A clustered pattern in a scatter graph is indicated when the dots are grouped together in little clusters, indicating that groups of places plotted on the graph all have similar features in common.

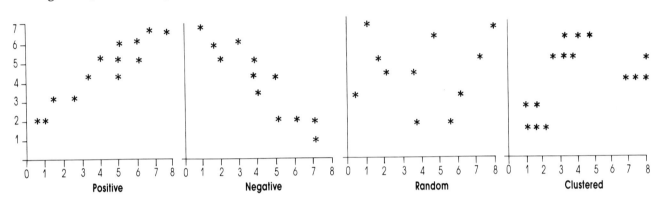

EXERCISES

Western Australia												
	Jan	Feb	Mar	Apr	May	June	July	Aug	Sept	Oct	Nov	Dec
Number of wet days	10	11	16	23	45	57	58	58	47	39	20	13
Number of hours of sun	320	280	270	220	180	140	160	190	210	250	290	320

1. Draw a scatter graph for the weather statistics shown in the table above.

2. Common sense tells us that if it is raining it is unlikely to be sunny! Work out the rank correlation coefficient for the average number of wet days and the average length of sunshine, month by month, in Western Australia. What can you deduce from your scatter graph and from the rank correlation coefficient?

3. Find or collect two sets of statistics to compare. Choose data which throw light on an aspect of the geography of your home area, county, or region. For instance, you could compare the *population* of towns in your area with the *number of A and B Class roads* leading to and from each town.

4. Draw a scatter graph to show the relationship between the two sets of data you have chosen.

5. Work out the rank correlation coefficient between the two sets of statistics.

6. What conclusions can you make after studying your scatter graph and the rank correlation coefficient?

PART 2: REFERENCE

This Reference section will assist you with your fieldwork and mapwork.

The sketch maps, drawings, photographs and tables have been designed to help you identify many of the geographical features you will see when you study the environment in the field and on large-scale maps. They will also jog your memory, suggesting some of the things you should be looking out for and helping you to recall the more detailed information you may already have studied.

GEOLOGY AND SCENERY

The geology of an area, that is the type of bedrock it has, affects the type of scenery and the use to which the land can be put. Tough *igneous rocks* (like granite and basalt) and *metamorphic rocks* (like slate and gneiss) often give rise to a bleak, sparsely populated, upland country inhabited mainly by sheep. Like some *sedimentary rocks*, such as many of the sandstones, these igneous and metamorphic rocks are not easily identified (for certain) on an Ordnance Survey map.

Ordnance Survey maps do provide clear evidence, however, of the presence of most of the limestones and (sometimes) of clay. Limestones are *permeable* or *pervious rocks*. This means that water soaks into the porous limestones like chalk, or through the cracks and crevices in jointed limestones, such as Carboniferous limestone.

The absence of water on the surface is, therefore, one of the most distinctive clues on the map to the possibility that limestone is the underlying bedrock. The absence of surface water has had a striking effect on the development of settlement patterns, since the first farmers needed accessible sources of water for their livestock and for their own needs. It was inconvenient to live on the chalk or limestone itself, so villages were built, instead, where the limestone (or chalk) joined other rocks and springs welled to the surface. Limestone and chalk uplands are still sparsely populated today, even though the land itself has been turned into good farmland.

The absence of streams, however, is not quite enough in itself to justify the conclusion that the rock below the surface must be chalk or limestone. It could be a sand which also soaks up water but creates a very different type of scenery from that of chalk or limestone, often pineland and heath.

Other rocks, notably clay, are impervious to water. These *impermeable rocks* (as they are called) do not let water pass through. Consequently their presence is often betrayed by a profusion of lakes, ponds, and streams on the surface, often in stark contrast to the absence of streams on the chalk or limestone hills close by.

In the illustrations on pages 87–9 you can see some of the clues which could help you to identify clay, chalk and Carboniferous limestone on an Ordnance Survey map.

Exposed rock face at a quarry

86

Clay

Clay is a soft rock which cannot support steep slopes. Consequently landforms in clay country tend to be smooth and either almost flat or gently sloping. Because clay is impermeable water stands on the surface. The presence of many streams, ponds, ditches and dykes are clues to the presence of clay. So, too, is an abundance of meadow and deciduous woodland, since both flourish on well-watered land. Farms on clay lands often have names featuring key words, such as Meadow Farm, Pasture Farm, Green Farm and Oak Farm. Since water is so easily accessible settlements are distributed right across the claylands, the only sparsely populated areas being those that are marshy, low-lying and subject to frequent floods.

Dairy farming predominates on clay since grassland flourishes on the rich, often waterlogged, soils. One of the principal uses for clay is as a raw material for bricks. This is why old brickworks and place names with brick in the title may offer a further clue.

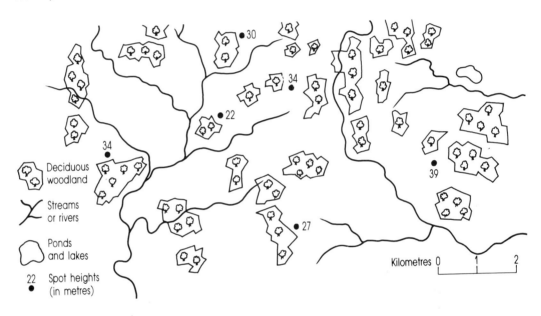

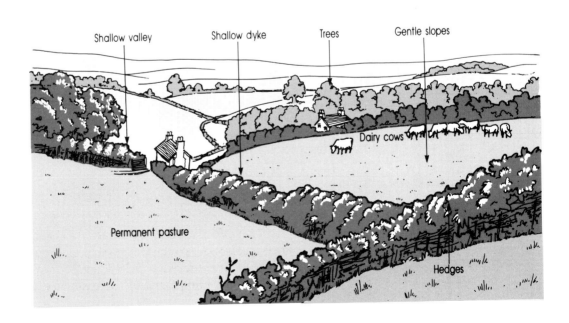

Chalk

Chalk is a harder rock than clay and consequently can support steeper slopes. These are softened by rainwater so that chalk hills and valleys tend to be gently rounded and smooth. The typical chalk landscape is undulating or rolling. The hills are rarely wooded. Any trees on a chalk upland usually grow on land where patches of clay lie on top of the chalk. Large pools, called *dewponds*, can also be found on some of these clay patches as well.

Five thousand years ago it was easier for primitive farmers to settle on the light woodlands of the chalk than in the thick forests on the lowland clays. Consequently, the presence of prehistoric features (such as Celtic Fields, tumuli, barrows, camps, carved figures in the white chalk, earthworks, stone circles) often provide clues which suggest that the underlying rock is probably chalk or a type of limestone.

Limestones are used in industry. This is why the presence of cement works and sometimes quarries can be an additional clue confirming that the bedrock is indeed a limestone. Place names, such as Chalk Hill, and dry valleys (see page 93) with names containing 'bourne', 'combe', 'coombe', or 'bottom' in them (e.g. Winterbourne, Long Combe, Winding Bottom) also help to identify chalk.

One of the most distinctive clues is the presence of many springs at the foot of a steep escarpment (see page 93), since this is invariably the site of a line of *spring-line settlements*. In the past the chalk downland was especially noted for its short grass and the sheep breeds (such as the Southdown) which thrived there. Nowadays many of the chalk lands have been ploughed up for cereals or provide pasture for cattle as well as sheep.

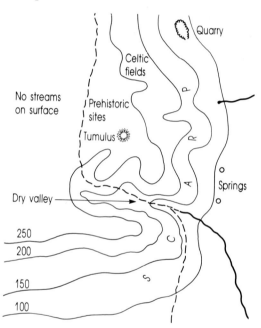

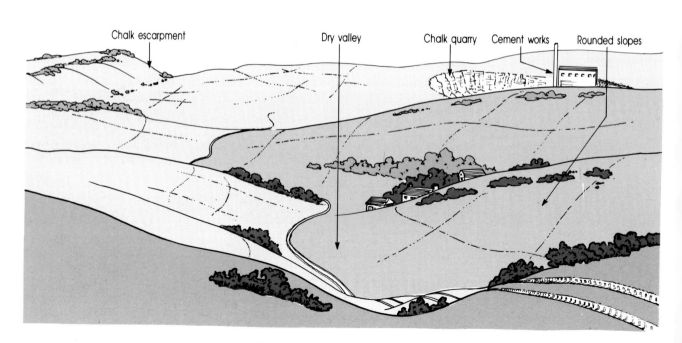

Carboniferous limestone

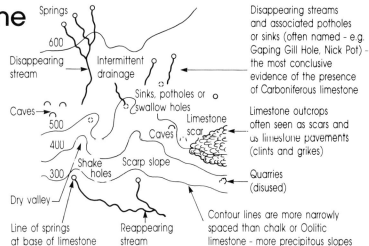

Carboniferous limestone is a tough, hard rock and where it occurs (or *outcrops*) at the surface it often leaves great scars and pavements of bare rock. There are few streams on the surface and, like chalk scenery, there are many dry valleys. However, the landscape of Carboniferous limestone country is more rugged than chalk and the slopes are often much steeper. This is why you can often find deep gorges marked on the map.

The most distinctive characteristic is the intermittent drainage system (see page 96) which is so common in Carboniferous limestone country. When rainwater absorbs chemicals from the air and from vegetation it turns into a mild form of acid. This acid reacts with the limestone to eat away at the cracks and joints in the rock to form deep fissures, called *grikes*. The limestone blocks in between these grikes are called *clints*. The grikes are gradually widened and allow the water on the surface to sink into the limestone where it eats away at the joints to form underground caverns. Streams disappear into these underground caves and caverns through distinctive holes which swallow them up, called *potholes*, *sinks*, or *swallow holes*. They often have unmistakeable names, such as Great Hard Pots, Stinking Holes, and Cow Pot. You can see many of them marked on the map on page 58.

The caverns underground often have limestone pillars hanging down from the roof like icicles (*stalactites*) and other pillars rising up from the floor (*stalagmites*). *Shake hole* is a Yorkshire term for *doline*, which is a hollow in the surface of the limestone caused by the collapse of a cavern roof underground.

The underground streams often reappear further down the valley as springs or as fully-fledged rivers.

Other clues include cement works, place names (such as Limekiln Pasture), disused quarries, and old lead mines. Carboniferous limestone country is hilly and sheep farming is common.

Other limestones in Britain include the oolitic limestone of the Cotswolds which is steeper and more rugged than chalk but not bleak and rock-scarred like Carboniferous limestone.

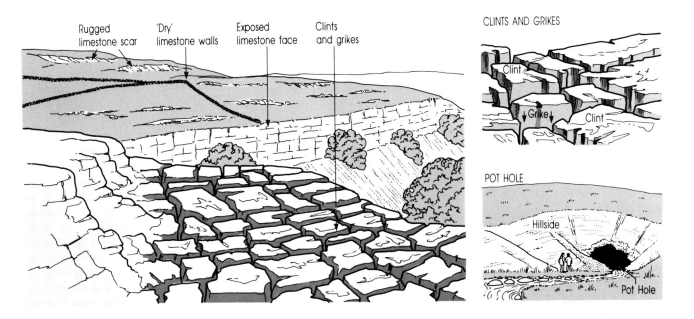

WEATHERING AND SOILS

Chemical weathering means the process by which chemical reactions break down solid rocks – the first stage in the process of soil formation. The results of chemical weathering are most obvious in areas of Carboniferous limestone where the reaction of acid rainwater with limestone has created clints, grikes, potholes, underground caverns, stalagmites and stalactites. In granite uplands chemical weathering may also have helped to form the characteristic granite tors which can be seen on some West Country moorlands, such as Dartmoor. Many other chemical reactions affect the minerals in rocks, helping to make them disintegrate into smaller pieces, such as the effects of water (e.g. hydrolysis and oxidation).

Granite tor on Dartmoor

Scree slope in the Lake District

Mechanical weathering, on the other hand, occurs when water freezes in the cracks in a rock face, causing fragments of rock to break off. These sharp-edged rock pieces collect on mountain sides as scree. Scree is sometimes marked on large-scale Ordnance Survey maps (as you can see in grid square 1572 on the map on page 56).

Weathering processes like these help to shape hillsides and provide the main material which other processes eventually turn into soils.

TESTING SOILS

Take a handful of soil and examine it carefully.

- Is the soil coarse and gritty to the touch?
  Does it include particles of sand?
  Is it impossible to make it stick together to form a ball? Does it leave the hand fairly clean after it has been handled?

If the answer is YES, the soil is probably SANDY

- Is the soil smooth and sticky when wet?
  Can it be easily shaped into a smooth round ball?
  Does it leave the hand dirty after it has been handled?

If the answer is YES, the soil is probably a CLAY

- Is the soil silky to the touch, neither coarse and gritty, nor smooth and sticky?
  Can it be shaped into a rather fragile ball?
  Does it leave the hand slightly soiled after being handled?

If the answer is YES, the soil is probably a LOAM

In practice, most soils fall in between these three categories, such as a sandy loam.

Reference: Weathering and Soils

If you see bare rock exposed, such as on a cliff side at the coast, or at the side of a river, you could measure the thickness of the different layers you see there and draw a simple soil profile, like the one in the diagram.

You can sometimes find evidence in the field of *soil erosion* (see also pages 126–7). In the Fenland region of East Anglia, the absence of hedges, trees and other windbreaks has sometimes meant that high winds have skimmed off fine dry soil from the vast, flat Fenland fields and piled it in heaps, like snowdrifts, in the roads running along the field boundaries.

You can also find evidence in the field of the movement of soil downhill (*soil creep*). This effect is particularly noticeable in photographs of the South Downs taken from the air. The whiteness of the underlying chalk shows through the fields at the top of a slope where the soil cover is thinner than at the bottom.

Dark brown soil with roots and decaying plants, worms and other creatures

Grey, sandy, lighter, coarser soil with stones and bits of rock

Weathered sandstone – the bedrock which has been broken up by the action of rain, frost, heat

Bedrock (the rock from which the soil has been formed)

A soil profile

Soil erosion

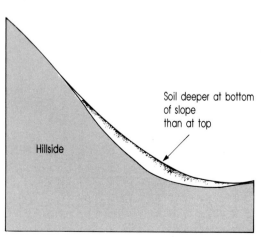
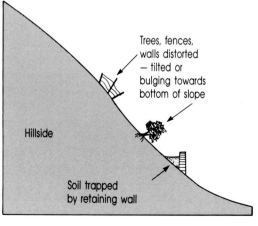

Two clues to the identification of soil creep

LANDFORMS ON AN ORDNANCE SURVEY MAP

These contour sketches show some of the principal contour patterns you should be able to locate and identify on a large-scale Ordnance Survey map.

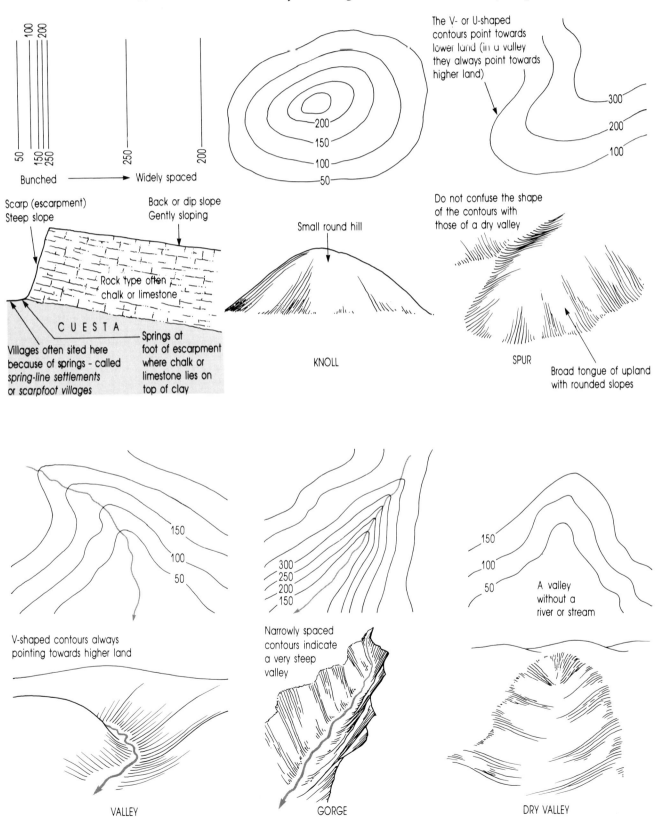

Reference: Landforms on an Ordnance Survey Map

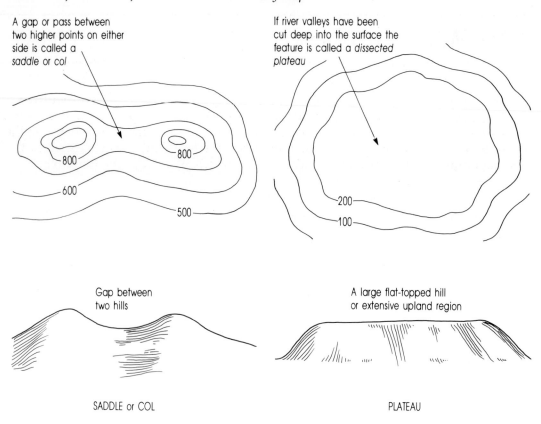

A gap or pass between two higher points on either side is called a *saddle or col*

If river valleys have been cut deep into the surface the feature is called a *dissected plateau*

Gap between two hills

A large flat-topped hill or extensive upland region

SADDLE or COL

PLATEAU

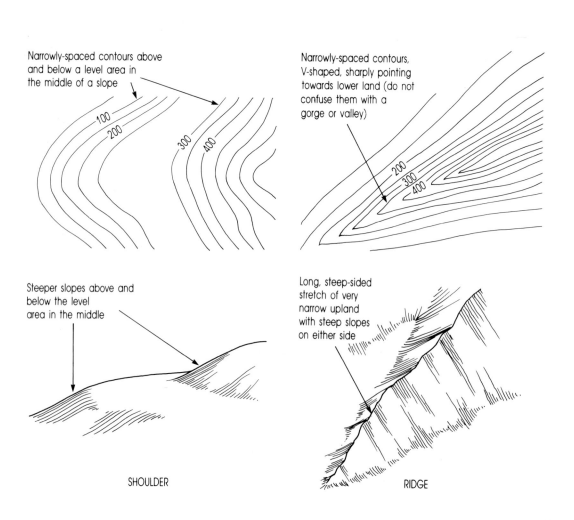

Narrowly-spaced contours above and below a level area in the middle of a slope

Narrowly-spaced contours, V-shaped, sharply pointing towards lower land (do not confuse them with a gorge or valley)

Steeper slopes above and below the level area in the middle

Long, steep-sided stretch of very narrow upland with steep slopes on either side

SHOULDER

RIDGE

THE WATER CYCLE

These diagrams illustrating the water cycle are greatly simplified, since water from lakes, rivers, ponds, streams, and from the earth itself, also evaporates, as well as the water in the sea. In addition, only part of the rainwater is returned immediately to the sea. Some is absorbed by the ground and raises the level of the water table whilst some evaporates long before it reaches the sea (such as water in the River Nile).

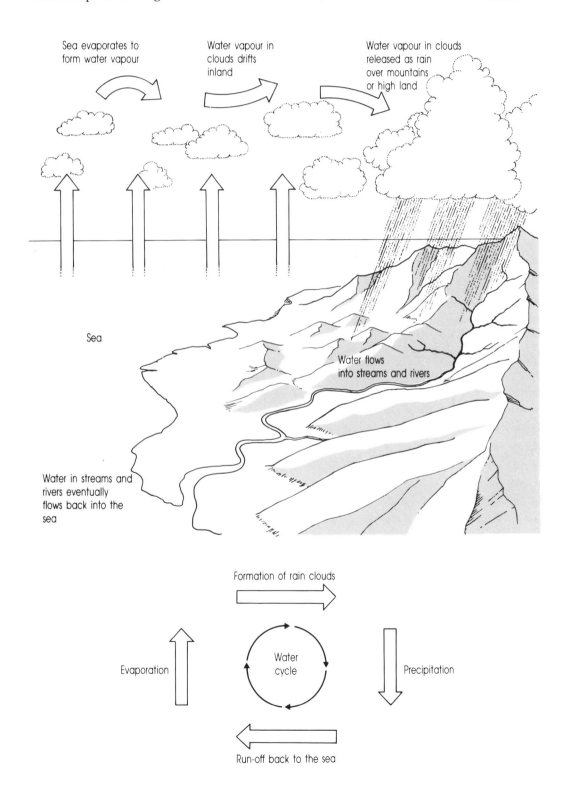

RIVERS

The *watershed* between two river drainage basins normally follows the crest of the hills or mountains separating them.

If you are asked to draw in the watershed between two or more river basins you can use the selective trace method (see page 73) to plot the river systems on the map. A drainage map like this makes it much easier to pick out the line of the watershed which can then be sketched in as a dotted line.

If you are asked to describe the drainage system on the map you could see, first of all, if it has a pattern similar to one of the sketch maps shown below.

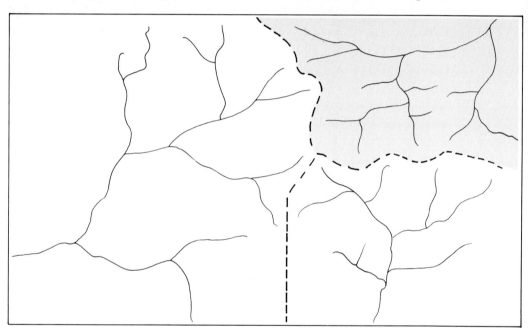

Watershed

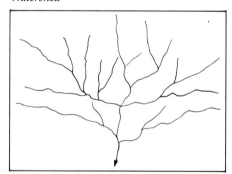

Dendritic drainage pattern

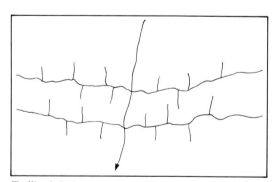

Trellised drainage pattern

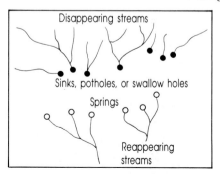

Intermittent drainage pattern

On this page, and pages 98–100, you can see contour sketches and illustrations depicting the main characteristics of river erosion and deposition and its effects on human geography. You should be able to identify some of these physical features on the Ordnance Survey map extracts on pages 56 and 58.

You will certainly be able to see some of the ways in which rivers and streams have affected the siting of settlements, such as the position of Ingleton (page 58) at the confluence of two rivers, the Doe and the Wiss, or the siting of Stronchreggan (grid square 0772) on a small delta jutting out into the loch on page 56.

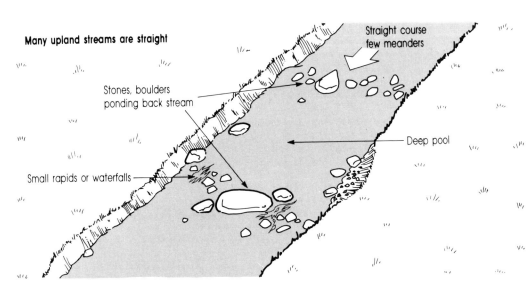

Upland river features (1)

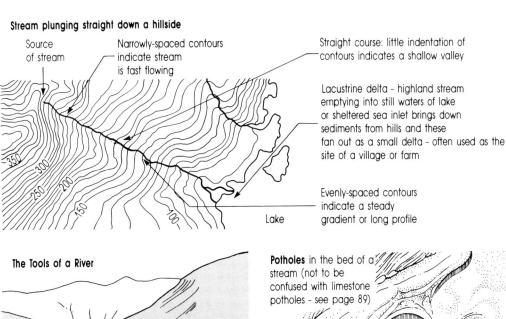

Upland river features (2)

Waterfall and Gorge

Deep V-shaped contours pointing sharply upstream indicate a deep-cut valley or gorge

Note the absence of a flood plain

The waterfall eats back into the highland so rapidly the valley sides left behind remain steep-sided – the sides of the gorge

Contours bunched together indicate a rapid fall in gradient – even if the waterfall was not marked we could suspect the presence of rapids and small falls

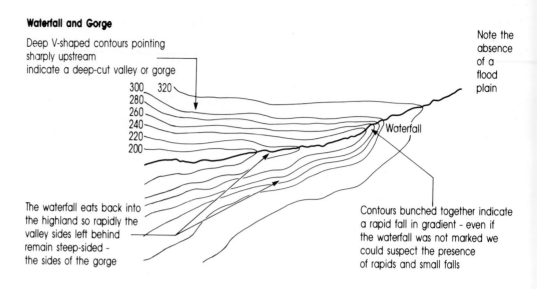

Features of a Waterfall

Waterfalls and gorges are likely sites for hydro-electric power schemes because of the force exerted by the river (the head of water) as it plunges over the waterfall

Fast, turbulent course pebble free

Relatively gentle course stones and pebbles

Waterfall

Hard rock

Some undercutting of cliff

Softer rock

Deep plunge pool

Gentle course – many stones and pebbles deposited

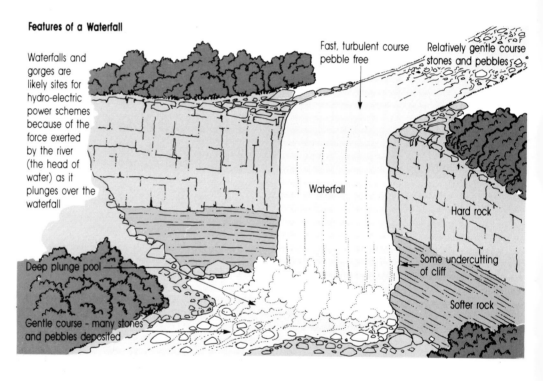

Interlocking Spurs

Where a swiftly meandering stream has cut deeply into the highland forming spurs which interlock together these are known as interlocking spurs

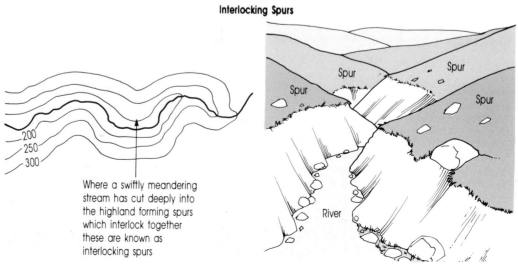

Rivers 99

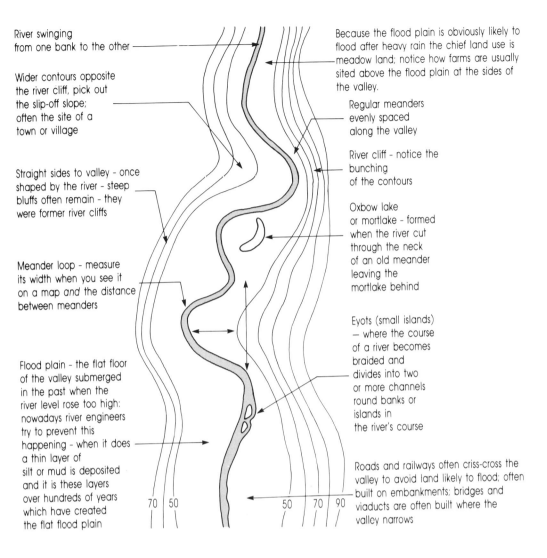

River meanders

River cliff and slip-off slope on the River Wye

Lowland river features

A Canalised River

Notice the very wide valley: absence of contours indicates a level flood plain — look out for spot heights

A canalised river is one that has been straightened and deepened and embankments built up to enable it to carry flood water away without spilling over on to the plain

Dykes, ditches, drains help to minimise the chances of flooding and enable the area to be used for farming - the farms however are above the flood plain

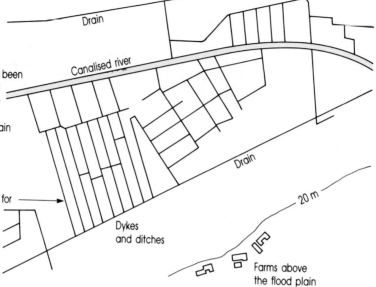

Levees or Embankments

Symbol for an embankment — almost always man-made although they are formed naturally on rivers not controlled by river engineers

Raised embankments on either side of a slow moving river

An Estuary

Channel cut by the river at low tide

Gradual widening of the estuary towards the mouth

Sand and mud deposited in the estuary mouth

Ground often marshy near the mouth of the river

Complete absence of contours indicates flat valley floor and land at sea-level

River channel at low tide

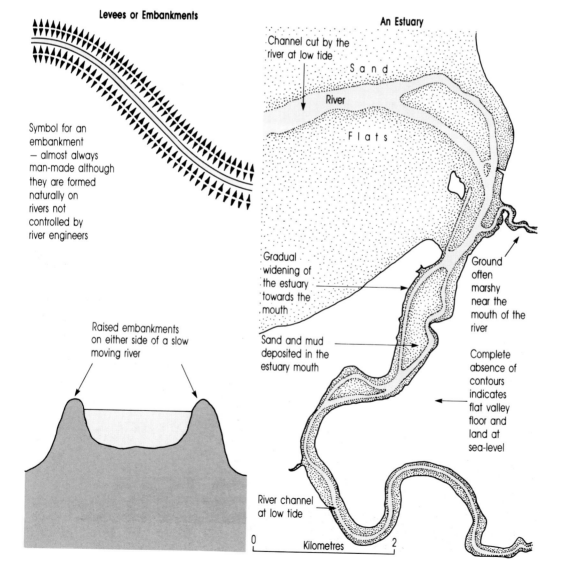

Rivers 101

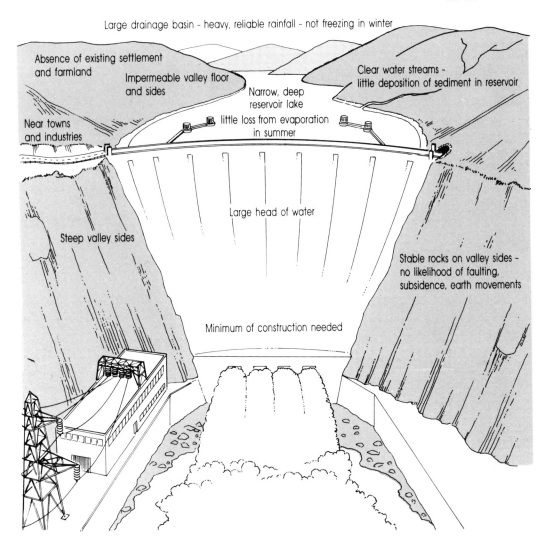

A hydro-electric scheme (highlighting the favourable factors sought by civil engineers looking for a new site for a dam, reservoir and power station)

How a river and its valley can be used

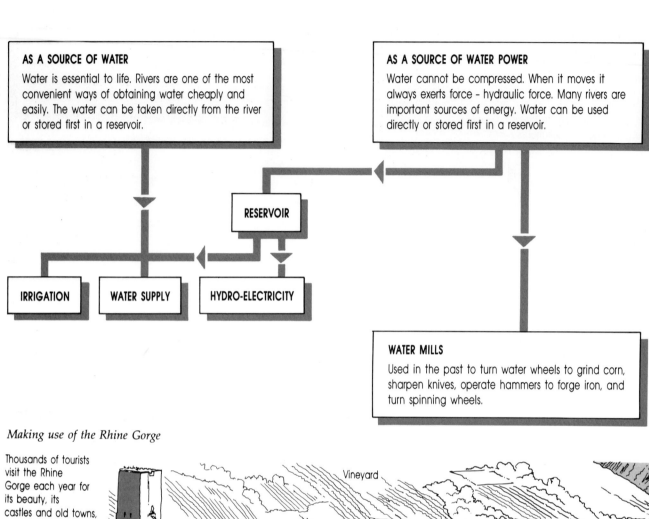

AS A SOURCE OF WATER
Water is essential to life. Rivers are one of the most convenient ways of obtaining water cheaply and easily. The water can be taken directly from the river or stored first in a reservoir.

AS A SOURCE OF WATER POWER
Water cannot be compressed. When it moves it always exerts force - hydraulic force. Many rivers are important sources of energy. Water can be used directly or stored first in a reservoir.

RESERVOIR

IRRIGATION

WATER SUPPLY

HYDRO-ELECTRICITY

WATER MILLS
Used in the past to turn water wheels to grind corn, sharpen knives, operate hammers to forge iron, and turn spinning wheels.

Making use of the Rhine Gorge

Thousands of tourists visit the Rhine Gorge each year for its beauty, its castles and old towns, and its wine

Vineyard

Main road and railway at the side of the valley carrying passengers and goods

Village on level ground at the bottom of the gorge in a side valley — hotels and restaurants for the tourists

A vineyard on the steep slopes of the gorge. Facing south, it gets the sun most of the day.

How a river and its valley can be used

AS A WASTE OUTLET
Many substances dissolve in water or can be held in suspension (like a medicine which is shaken). Water also dilutes liquids. This is why rivers flowing to the sea are used as drains to carry away waste products - a major source of pollution.

AS A ROUTEWAY
Roads, railways and canals follow valleys as routeways because the river has cut a wide or deep gap through the higher land to form a natural cutting.

USING THE VALLEY

USING THE RIVER

USED AS A DRAIN
Using water power to transport sewage, industrial effluent and other waste products downstream to the mouth of the river.

Inland waterways
Some rivers are used directly by barges and river steamers.

Estuaries
Sheltered waterways are ideal for seaports.

ROADS — RAILWAYS — CANALS — RIVER TRAFFIC — SHIPPING

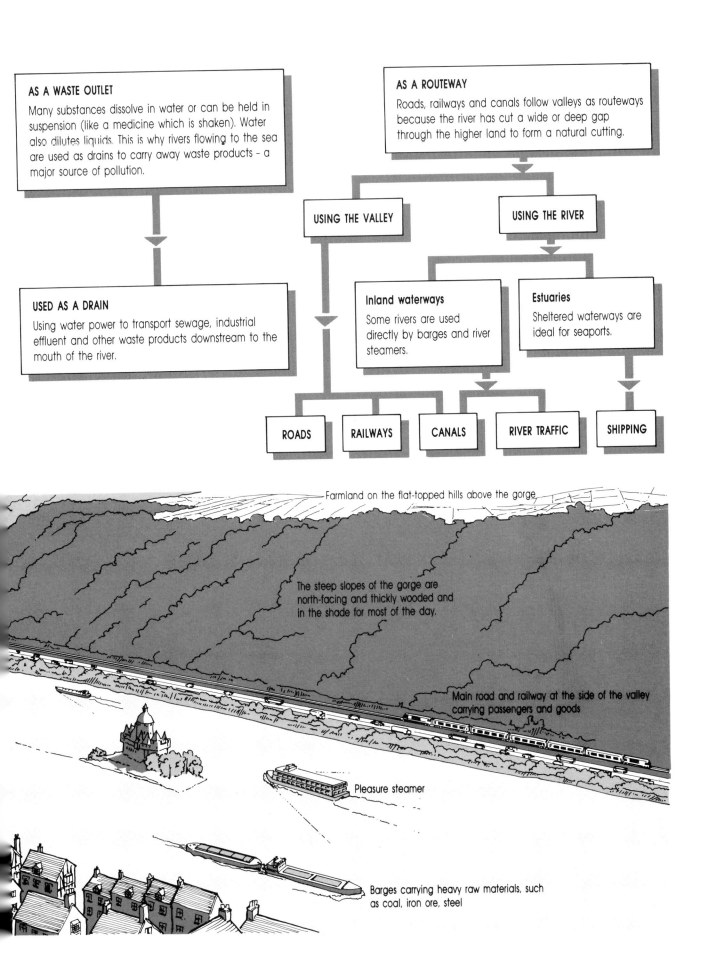

Farmland on the flat-topped hills above the gorge

The steep slopes of the gorge are north-facing and thickly wooded and in the shade for most of the day.

Main road and railway at the side of the valley carrying passengers and goods

Pleasure steamer

Barges carrying heavy raw materials, such as coal, iron ore, steel

COASTLINES

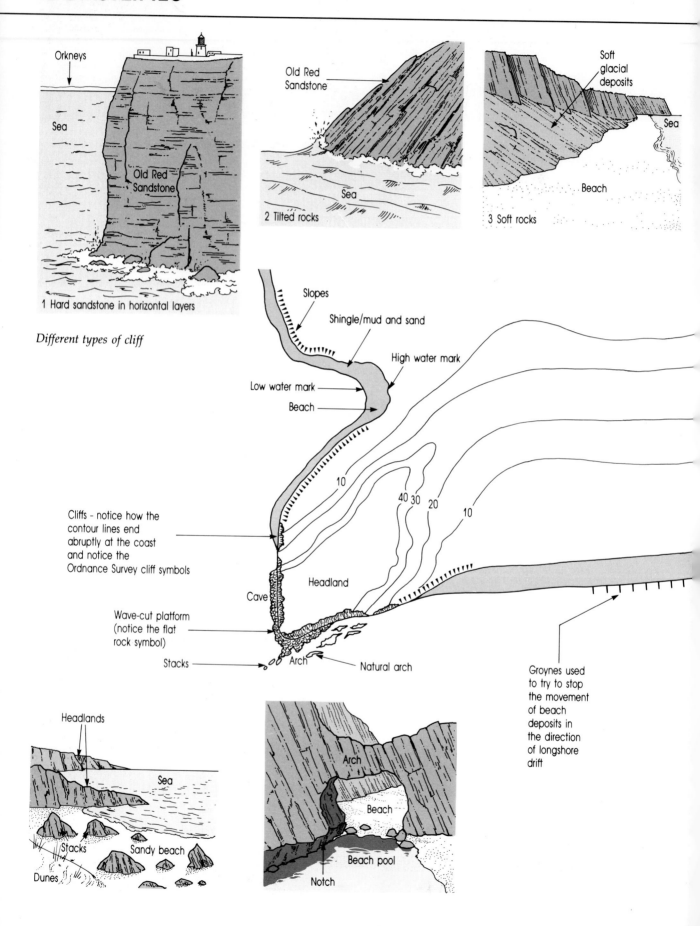

Different types of cliff

Spit at Spurn Head, Humberside

Offshore bar, Scolt Head Island off the north Norfolk coast

Coastal plain (almost flat)

Salt marshland

Inlets left high and dry at low tide

Notice the recurved tip of the offshore bar and the mud/sand banks extending beyond it

Spit diverting the mouth of a river

River channel at low tide

Offshore bar - an island built up by deposition

Salt marsh, Canvey Island, Essex

On the 1:25 000 series much greater detail shown such as dunes, separate symbols for mud, sand, sand and shingle. Also low water marked in light blue, high water marked in deeper blue.

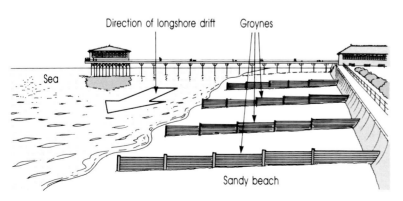

Direction of longshore drift · Groynes · Sea · Sandy beach

Rias, fjords and raised beaches

Sea-level does not remain constant. When it rises (because of melting ice sheets for example) or, conversely, when earth movements cause the land surface to sink, the sea *drowns* the low-lying land at the coast. It submerges some existing islands and sometimes creates new ones.

Two of the most distinctive features formed at the coast by such a rise in sea-level are *rias* (drowned river valleys and estuaries) and *fjords* (drowned glaciated valleys). Both make excellent sites for seaports because they are deep-water anchorages. Because of their scenic beauty they also attract tourists. Rias can be seen in the south-western peninsulas of the British Isles – in Devon and Cornwall, in south-west Wales, and in south-west Ireland – and also in the west-facing European peninsulas, such as Brittany in France. European fjords are found mainly in western Norway and north-western Scotland.

When sea-level falls (or conversely when earth movements cause the land surface to rise) former beaches at the coast are raised above the sea level as terraces. *Raised beaches* like these can be seen along many of the coasts of Scotland. Because the raised beach is flat it is almost always used as farmland in an area where level land suitable for farming is scarce (see also page 36).

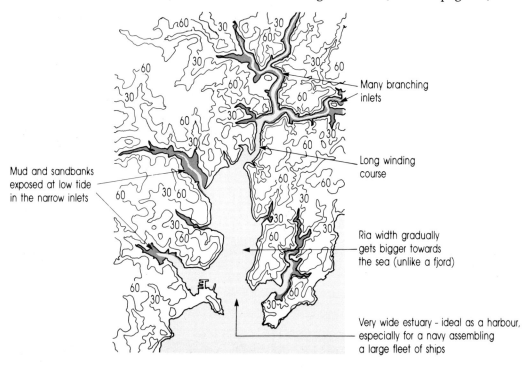

A ria

A ria, St Just, Cornwall

Rias, fjords and raised beaches 107

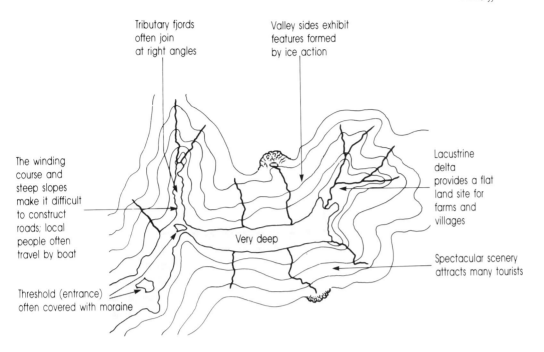

A fjord

Fjord or sea loch, Loch Hourn in north-west Scotland

Raised beach at Shieldaig in north-west Scotland. Notice the linear shape of the village (see page 117)

GLACIATION

Glaciers create many different landforms. Some can be easily identified on a large-scale Ordnance Survey map. Others can only be seen clearly on the ground or in a photograph. In the drawings below you can see the effect of glaciation upon a lowland area, such as the floor of a valley, which was covered by a glacier, or ice sheet, during the Ice Age.

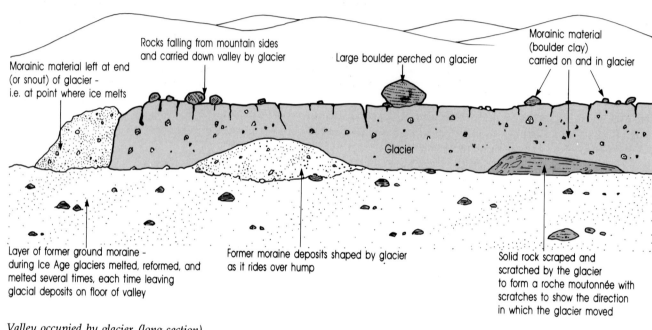

Valley occupied by glacier (long section)

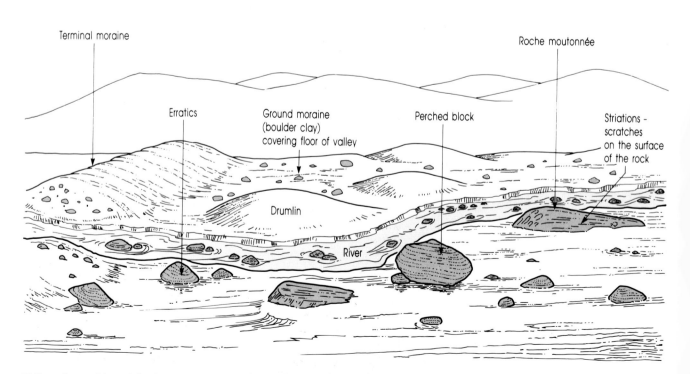

Valley after melting of the ice

Living in a glaciated valley

The drawing below and the photographs on page 110–11 show some of the ways in which glaciation affects the lives of the people who live in glaciated valleys in mountain regions, such as the Alps. Although farming is an important activity in the valleys of the Alps, the most important source of income is tourism. Holidaymakers are attracted to the Alps in winter for the skiing and in summer for the walks, views, and clear mountain air. Glaciation has increased the attraction of the valleys for tourists because it has created a landscape of steep overhanging valley sides with many waterfalls (hanging valleys). It has created many long finger, or ribbon, lakes which are ideal for recreations such as sailing. It has also etched jagged deep-set *corries* into the mountain sides with steep ridges (*arêtes*) between them and peaks shaped like pyramids (called *horns* – as in the Matterhorn).

Despite the wealth that tourism brings to the valleys of the Alps, and to similar valleys in the English Lake District, Snowdonia, south-western Ireland, Scotland and Norway, the use of the mountains as skiing and holiday resorts has created many problems as well. The traditional ways of life have suffered as farms have been turned into camp sites and caravan centres or the land used for building hotels, motels, and holiday homes.

Conservationists are disturbed by the damage done to mountain tracks by thousands of climbers each year. Roads and other services in the mountain areas are often congested in the holiday months. The conflicts within these mountain regions are further aggravated by the use made of the high rainfall of these regions to supply water to major cities some distance away, such as from Loch Katrine to Glasgow and from Thirlmere to Manchester.

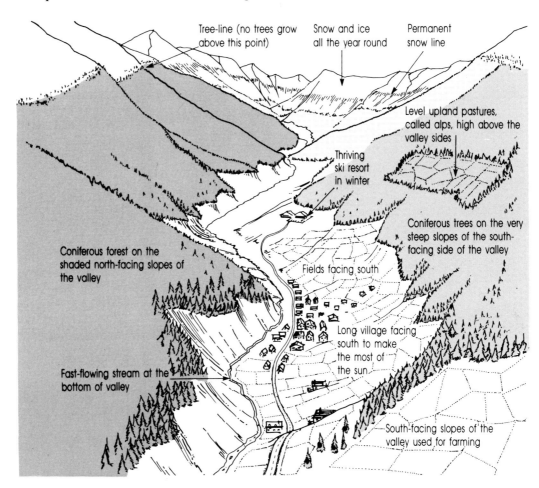

Glaciated valley in the Alps

A glaciated valley on the map

Striding Edge (an arête) and Red Tarn in a corrie on the flanks of Helvellyn in the English Lake District

CIRQUE, CWM, or CORRIE
An armchair hollow cut into the side of a hill or mountain with a steep, scree-covered, rock cliff at the back (the backwall) and also on either side. Indicated by narrowly-spaced, C-shaped contours on the map, usually marked by the symbol for bare rock. Often with a small lake or tarn in the centre.

CORRIE TARN
A small lake in a hollow in a corrie, often dammed up by moraine. The fact that there used to be a tarn in the corrie is often indicated by the symbol for marsh, showing that the land is still very damp.

SCREE
Rock which has been broken off the rock face by frost action. Often shown on a map by dots. (See also page 90).

DRUMLINS
Long elongated mounds filled with moraine, sometimes shown on a map by closed oval contours.

Drumlin near Grasmere, Cumbria

LACUSTRINE DELTAS
Finger lakes are usually in the process of being filled in by mountain streams. These bring down sediment eroded from the mountains. The sediment forms lake (lacustrine) deltas. Shown on the map as small triangles of land jutting out into the lake. Often used for agriculture.

A glaciated valley on the map

ARÊTE
A steep-sided ridge between two corries. Where two or more arêtes have receded towards each other they sometimes form a *pyramidal peak* or *horn* (named after the celebrated Matterhorn in Switzerland).

TRUNCATED SPUR
These are spurs of land with steep rather than rounded slopes lining the sides of the valley. They were cut back (truncated) by the glacier as it forced its way down the valley.

U-SHAPED VALLEY
Narrowly-spaced contours (steep slopes) on either side of a flat valley floor (no contours). The valley floor is flat because it was once a lake and has since been filled in with sediment brought down by mountain streams.

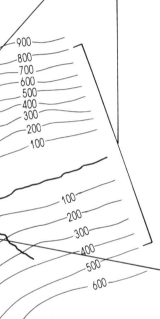

U-shaped valley at Grasmere, Cumbria. The flat valley floor of many glaciated valleys is used for settlement, agriculture, and communications.

HANGING VALLEY
A waterfall or stream plunging down the side of a U-shaped valley. Shown on the map by streams cutting across narrowly-spaced contours (little or no V-shape, see page 97).

Hanging valley in the Lauterbrunnen Valley in Switzerland

RIBBON or FINGER LAKE
Long, thin, narrow lakes in hollows gouged out and overdeepened by a former glacier or dammed up by a terminal moraine. Used by tourists (where permitted) for fishing, steamer trips, sailing, water skiing, wind surfing, and other water sports.

Finger lake near Bettyhill in northern Scotland

FARMING

INPUTS

Climate and weather Rainfall; temperature; snowfall; sunshine; possible effects of frost and wind.

Relief - height above sea level. Slope of land (easy, hard, or difficult to plough?). **Aspect** - fields facing south (sunny) or north (shaded)? Small fields?

Soils Acid or alkaline? Deep or shallow? Sandy, loam, or clay? Lacking humus?

Drainage Dry or wet land? Drain pipes under the main fields?

Existing buildings on the farm can only be used for specialised types of farming (e.g. dairying unit). This may make it hard for the farmer to change to new types of farming.

New machinery and technology (e.g. microcomputers)

Capital (money) available to buy livestock, machinery, seed, new buildings, etc.

Sources of energy available on the farm. Some isolated farms rely on their own generators. Many use bottled gas.

Workers At some times of the year (e.g. lambing) there is too much work to do. At other times there is too little.

Seed - the essential input on any farm growing crops.

Quality livestock from which to breed.

The Common Agricultural Policy of the European Community makes it possible for farmers (e.g. hill sheep farmers) to prosper under circumstances which would otherwise make it hard for them to survive.

Willingness to adopt new methods and experiment with new crops, fertilisers, crop sprays, and new breeds of livestock.

Fertilisers and pesticides

Farming 113

PROCESSES

Breeding Lambing; calving; animal care and selection; feeding and grazing livestock.

Collecting ongoing livestock products; milking cows, shearing sheep, collecting eggs.

Storing crops and livestock products; distribution and sale.

Cultivating the soil: ploughing, discing, harrowing; sowing seed.

Nurturing and protecting growing crops; spraying pesticides; irrigation.

Making silage and hay; harvesting corn and roots; cutting vegetables; picking fruit; etc.

Manuring Storing and spreading livestock manure; spreading lime and fertilisers; etc.

OUTPUTS

Edible livestock products Milk, butter, cheese, cream, beef cattle, fat lambs, mutton, pork pigs, bacon pigs, poultry, eggs.

Live animals Calves, bulls, cows, heifers, breeding ewes, rams, sows, boars, horses, day-old chicks, etc.

Crops Hay; silage; cereals - wheat, barley, oats; root crops - potatoes, sugar beet, turnips; clover, grasses.

Market gardening Vegetables - peas, carrots, beans, sprouts; soft fruits - strawberries; orchard fruits - apples, pears, cherries, plums; flowers; herbs.

By-products Animal manure; straw; wool; hides, leathers, skins.

INDUSTRY

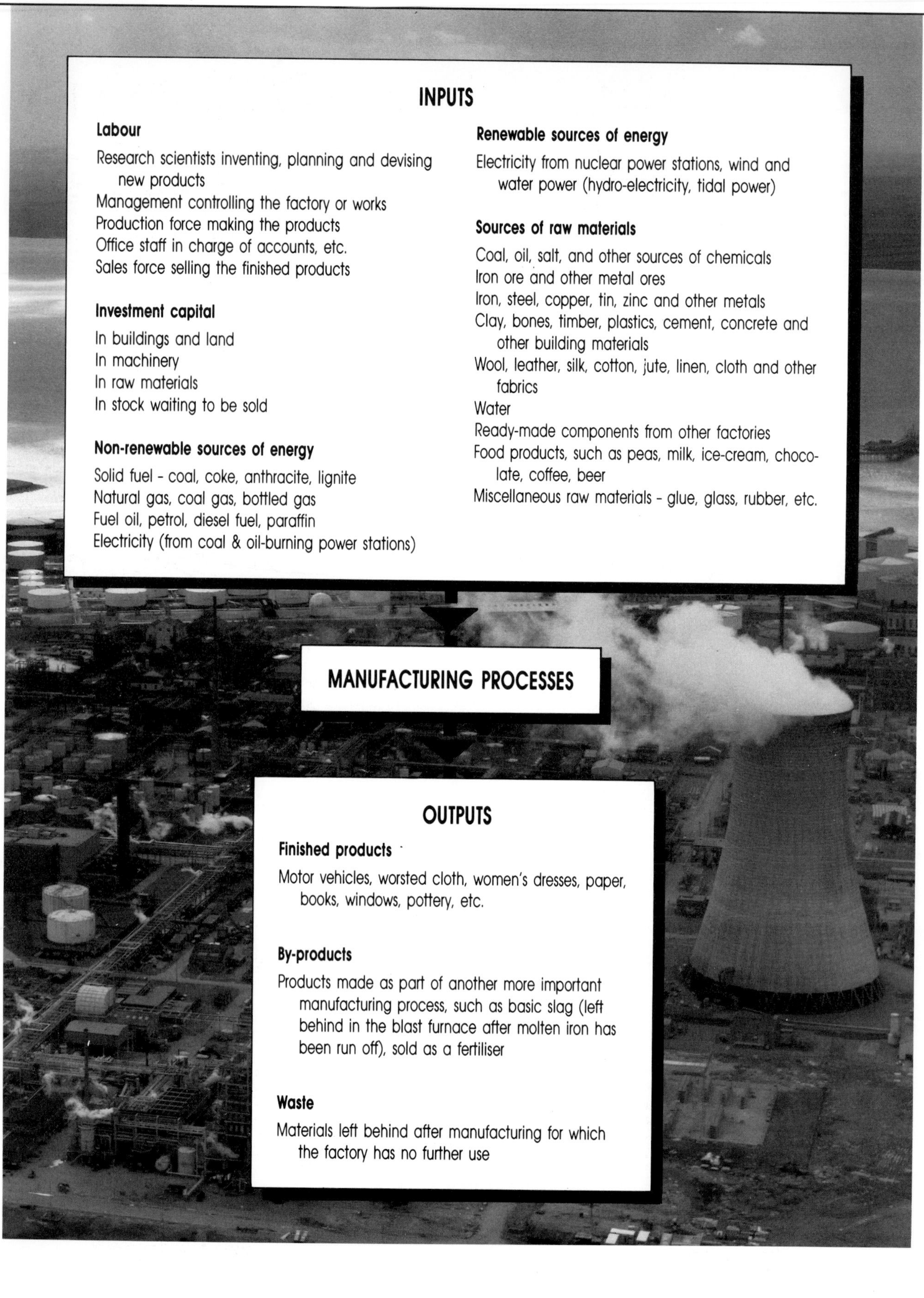

INPUTS

Labour

Research scientists inventing, planning and devising new products
Management controlling the factory or works
Production force making the products
Office staff in charge of accounts, etc.
Sales force selling the finished products

Investment capital

In buildings and land
In machinery
In raw materials
In stock waiting to be sold

Non-renewable sources of energy

Solid fuel – coal, coke, anthracite, lignite
Natural gas, coal gas, bottled gas
Fuel oil, petrol, diesel fuel, paraffin
Electricity (from coal & oil-burning power stations)

Renewable sources of energy

Electricity from nuclear power stations, wind and water power (hydro-electricity, tidal power)

Sources of raw materials

Coal, oil, salt, and other sources of chemicals
Iron ore and other metal ores
Iron, steel, copper, tin, zinc and other metals
Clay, bones, timber, plastics, cement, concrete and other building materials
Wool, leather, silk, cotton, jute, linen, cloth and other fabrics
Water
Ready-made components from other factories
Food products, such as peas, milk, ice-cream, chocolate, coffee, beer
Miscellaneous raw materials – glue, glass, rubber, etc.

MANUFACTURING PROCESSES

OUTPUTS

Finished products

Motor vehicles, worsted cloth, women's dresses, paper, books, windows, pottery, etc.

By-products

Products made as part of another more important manufacturing process, such as basic slag (left behind in the blast furnace after molten iron has been run off), sold as a fertiliser

Waste

Materials left behind after manufacturing for which the factory has no further use

Industrial changes

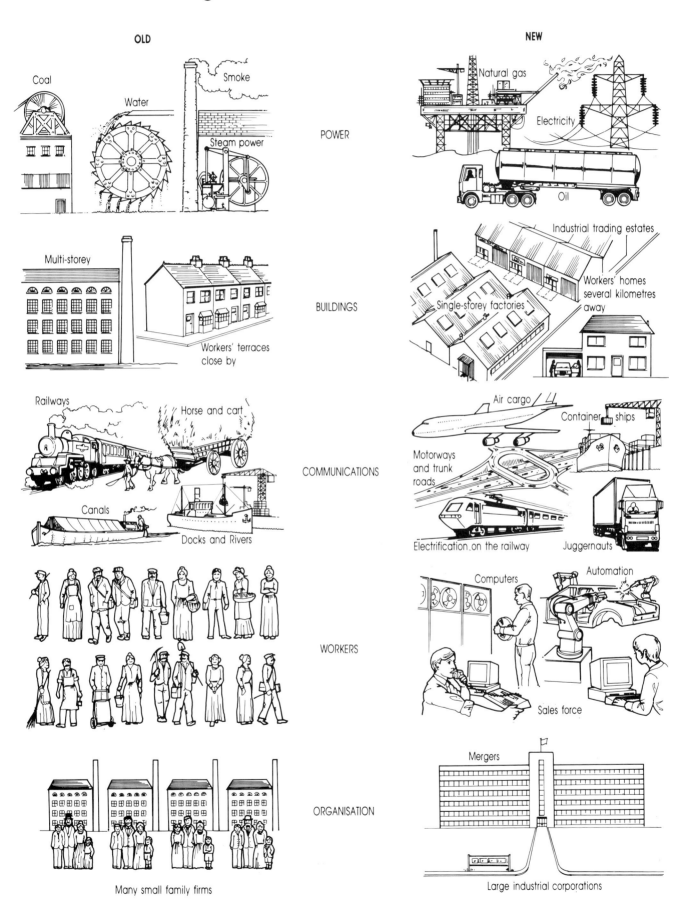

Industrial sites on an Ordnance Survey map

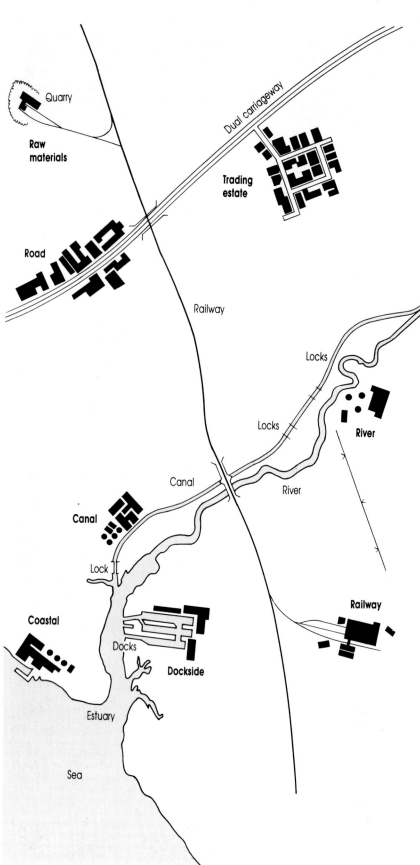

Location of industries depends upon:

- whether suitable land as a site for the factory buildings is available;
- whether the required energy sources are readily and cheaply available;
- accessibility to raw materials/ components;
- an efficient transport system;
- being able to obtain the required labour supply – skilled, semi-skilled, non-skilled;
- whether there are similar or related industries in the same area – if there are, then it will be easier to recruit skilled labour, easier to assemble raw materials, easier to distribute the finished products;
- personal decisions made by the owners and directors;
- EEC, central and local government policy which may (or may not) encourage the building of a new factory or works in the area in order to help solve local unemployment problems:
  by subsidies,
  by generous loans at low rates of interest,
  by cheap building sites, etc;
- industrial inertia – the fact that an area has always produced a certain product (e.g. Stoke-on-Trent and the pottery industry) – one incentive is that new products will benefit from the reputation of the local product for quality (such as Sheffield steel).

SETTLEMENTS

The original site and shape of a modern town is sometimes hard to identify on a map. This is partly because the later growth of modern housing estates and suburbs produces a confusing pattern on the map which may obscure the original heart of the town. In addition, redevelopment of the town centre at successive times in the past, as well as at the present, may also have obliterated evidence which could define the first settlement on the site. In the countryside, however, the settlement shapes on this page can often be identified in many villages and small towns.

Linear Shapes

Along a road

Along the coast

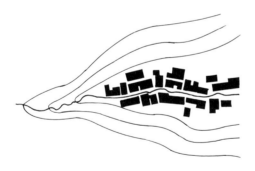

In a deep-cut valley

Along a road junction

Cluster Shapes

Cross-shaped road junctions

Village greens

Clustered round a castle, church, cathedral, abbey

Growth of a town

OLD TOWN (BEFORE 1837)

ON THE MAP

Some old towns grew up around an abbey or castle

Cathedral

Blocked in area of streets: no regular pattern

Churches with towers or steeples

Medieval houses

Georgian houses

IN THE FIELD

In some well-preserved towns with a long history, such as Norwich, you can often find evidence of building from many different periods. In York you could plot on a map buildings from the Roman, Viking, and medieval periods as well as the seventeenth, eighteenth, nineteenth and twentieth centuries. In new towns, however, only a few buildings (such as the parish church) are likely to be older than 1837.

VICTORIAN (1837-1901)

ON THE MAP

Works

Works

Before the coming of cheap public transport workers had to live within walking distance of the factories and mills

Rectangular grid of streets (bends not necessary before motor vehicles)

Railway station on fringe of town in 1850s or whenever it was built stimulated growth of town close to station

Mid-nineteenth-century

Late-nineteenth-century

IN THE FIELD

The age of Victorian buildings is often given away by dates on headstones above the main entrance of a building, on foundation stones, and on plaques. Street names also provide a clue, such as those named after events (Omdurman Terrace after the battle of Omdurman fought in 1898) or after people (such as Nightingale Street after Florence Nightingale at the time of the Crimean War between 1854 and 1856).

TWENTIETH CENTURY (1901 TO PRESENT DAY)

ON THE MAP

Curved streets

Cul-de-sacs

Housing estates often filling in gaps between main roads

Less densely built up than in Victorian streets

Carefully planned

Edwardian (c.1905)

1920s and 1930s

Postwar 1960s

IN THE FIELD

Edwardian houses often had large ornate bay windows on the ground floor and on the first floor. Street and house names often reveal dates, such as those named after Boer War battles and generals (e.g. Buller, Colenso, Mafeking, Ladysmith).

Houses in the 1920s and 1930s are usually easy to date. Many of these houses also have bay windows. They often have one or two small stained glass or circular windows, have walls covered with pebble dash, and sometimes feature black timber beams under the gables to look like those on medieval buildings (see opposite). Names are sometimes a clue, such as King George V Avenue (1910-36) or Jubilee Avenue (1935).

Postwar buildings are easiest of all to spot, partly because they look new, and have plain fronts compared with those of the 1920s and 1930s. They tend to have large picture windows or mock-Georgian windows and usually have less-mature gardens (often open plan) than the houses built between the wars. Names are sometimes a clue, such as John F Kennedy Avenue.

A typical town

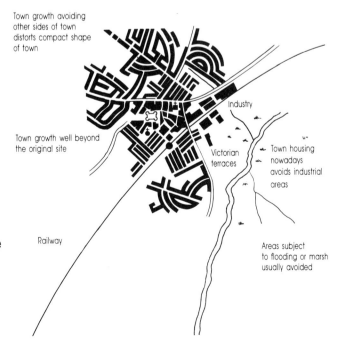

Town growth avoiding other sides of town distorts compact shape of town

Town growth well beyond the original site

Railway

Cheap public transport and motor cars make it easy to live some distance from the town centre

Industry

Victorian terraces

Town housing nowadays avoids industrial areas

Areas subject to flooding or marsh usually avoided

Town sites

If you are asked to analyse the site of a town from map evidence:

1. Try to identify the original centre of the settlement.
2. Look at the contour lines and at the position of the town site in relation to the nearest river and surrounding hills.
3. Try to picture the landscape of this area several hundred years ago. What advantages did this site possess over other sites in the vicinity? To answer this question you will have to imagine a time:

- when a defensive site was an advantage;
- when a horse and cart or a boat were the only ways of moving heavy goods across Britain;
- when there were relatively few roads and bridges;
- when there was no mains water supply on tap;
- when many rivers were wider and shallower than they are today;
- when valleys were frequently marshy and subject to regular floods.

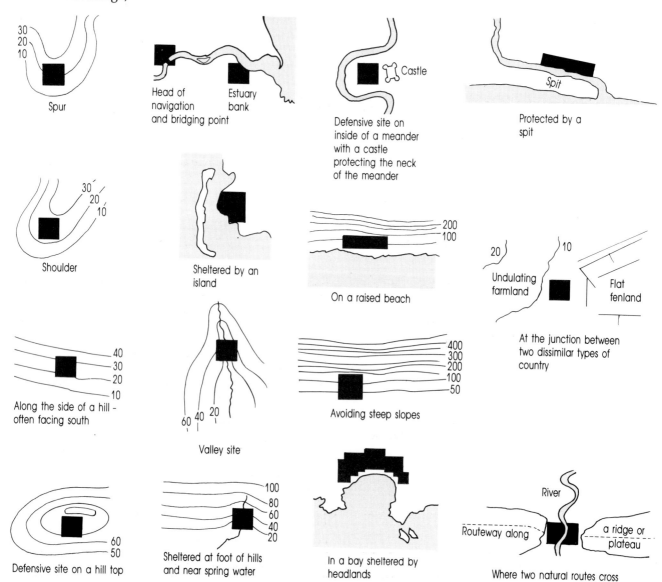

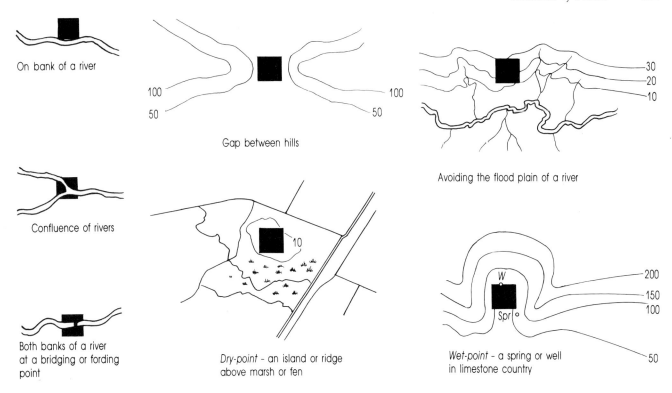

Functions of a town

All towns are towns because they perform functions which can only be performed in a centre within easy reach of the people living in the vicinity of the town. You can locate some of these functions on a large-scale map or plan, such as the position of a cathedral or town hall. But many functions can only be identified in the field, plotting the function of each building on a large-scale plan or street map.

Classify the buildings you see under one of the following headings:

Administrative centre	Government offices (Inland Revenue, DSS, Department of Health), local council offices, law courts, police
Commercial centre	Banks, building societies, insurance
Shopping centre	Department stores, chain stores, individual shops
Transport and communications centre	Railway station, bus station, airport, ring road, motorway link road, car parks, radio and television stations, post office
Social, leisure and recreation centre	Sports centre, league football, parks, restaurants, cinemas, theatres, swimming pool, nightclubs, public houses, religious buildings
Tourist or holiday centre	Pier, promenade, Winter Gardens, bandstand, hotels, conference centre
Services centre	Hospitals, doctors, dentists, ambulances, vet, schools, colleges, university, museum
Residential centre	Houses, blocks of flats, retirement homes

Urban hierarchies and hinterlands

Type of settlement	Social, leisure and recreational	Transport and communications	Shopping	Administrative
Hamlet		Telephone box Filling station	Travelling shop	
Village or suburb	Meeting hall Playing field Public house Swings/slides Fish and chip shop	Telephone exchange Road junction Service station	General store Sub post office Newsagent Food shop(s)	Parish council
Town or suburban centre	Cinema Sports centre Nightclub/disco League football Small theatre Restaurants and cafes Hotel	Bus station Railway station Radio station Local airport Taxi services Weekly newspaper Bypass	Chain stores (e.g. Boots/Woolworth) Clothing, shoe, and wine shops Head post office Supermarkets Book shop	Council offices Inland Revenue Job Centre DSS offices Department of Health Mayor
City or large town	Skating rink Concert hall County cricket Two or more theatres Two or more cinemas Many hotels and restaurants	Television station Daily/evening paper Ring road Special motorway link roads International airport	Large department stores Large record stores Branches of all chain stores	County hall City hall Lord Mayor Chief Education Officer
Metropolis	Many theatres Opera house National sports stadiums Many big luxury hotels	Railway terminus for all services Focus of motorways	Most exclusive fashion shops in the country	Seat of national government Civil service headquarters

Commercial	Services	Possible ways of measuring its sphere of influence or urban hinterland	Type of settlement
	Mobile library		**Hamlet**
Bank	Primary school Village church Doctor Nurse	Plotting on a map the homes of children attending the village school Distance from other villages	**Village or suburb**
Several banks Building societies Insurance brokers Solicitors	Secondary school Technical college Several churches and chapels Dentist Museum Hospital Branch library	Plotting on a map the out-of-town advertisers in the local paper Area served by the hospital, technical college, television rental firms, radio station Distance from similar towns	**Town or suburban centre**
Regional offices and headquarters of banks and many other businesses	University Cathedral Polytechnic Mosque/synagogue/temple Art gallery Teaching hospital Large reference library	Plotting on a map the out-of-town advertisers in the local daily/evening papers Area served by regional headquarters of banks and other large businesses Distance from similar cities	**City or large town**
Headquarters of national banks and major companies Stock Market	Universities Cathedrals National museums and art galleries	Distance from metropolitan centres of comparable importance	**Metropolis**

POLLUTION AND CONSERVATION

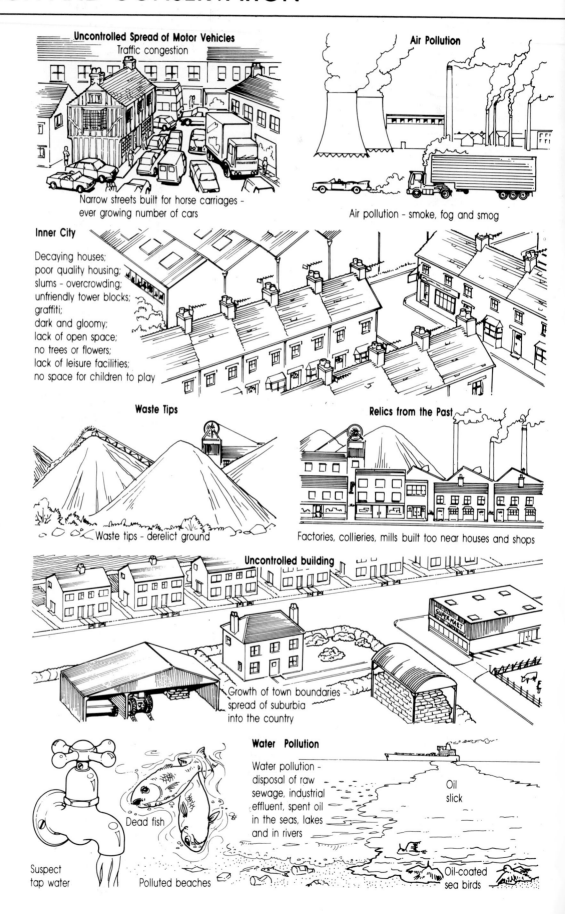

Pollution and conservation

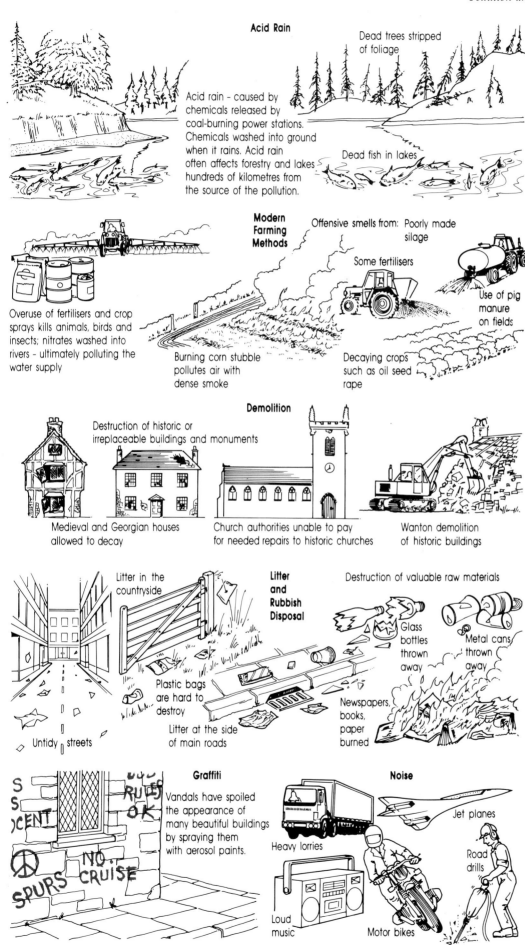

Soil erosion

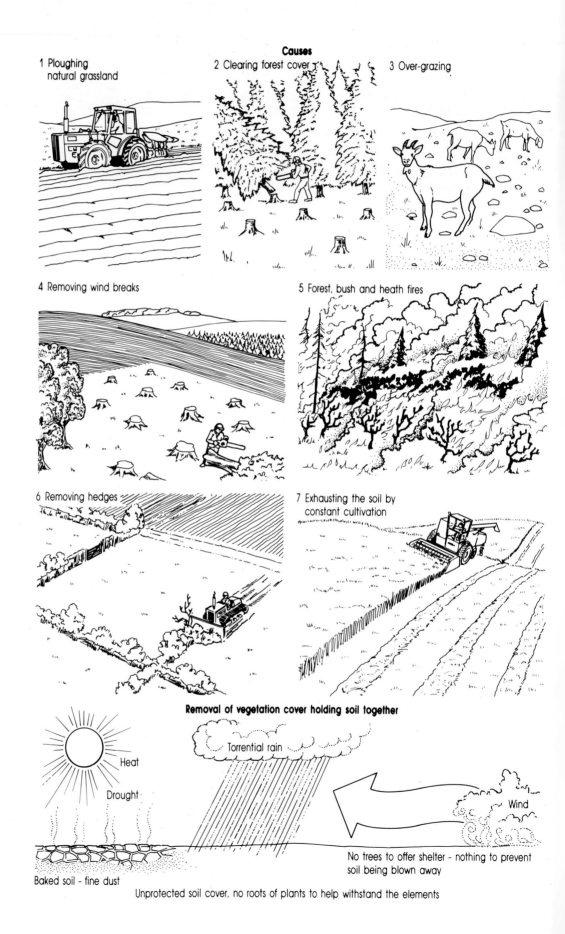

Soil erosion

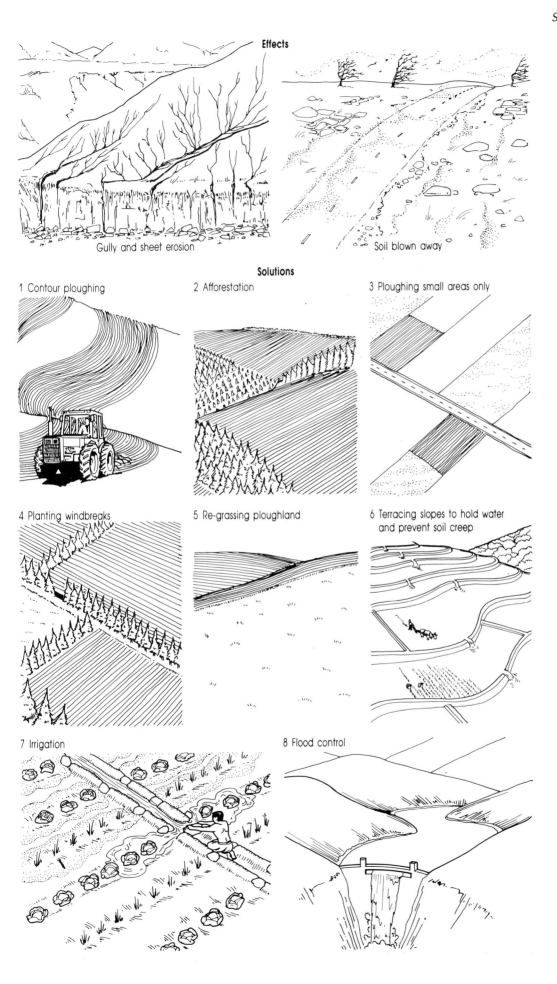

Effects
Gully and sheet erosion
Soil blown away

Solutions
1 Contour ploughing
2 Afforestation
3 Ploughing small areas only
4 Planting windbreaks
5 Re-grassing ploughland
6 Terracing slopes to hold water and prevent soil creep
7 Irrigation
8 Flood control

INDEX

abbreviations on a map 39, 53
aerial photographs 57, 59, 60, 63
age–sex pyramid 79
ages of buildings 118–19
amenity index 34
angle of view 60–1
annotated maps 39
area, estimating 70–1
arithmetic mean 81
averages 77, 81

bar graph 79
buildings 9–10, 12, 16, 23, 113, 115, 118–19, 124–5

Carboniferous limestone 58–9, 89, 90
Central Business District 9–10
chalk 88
chemical weathering 90, 125
choropleth maps 72
clay 87
climate 6, 78, 80, 83–5, 113
climograph 78
clinometer 31
cluster patterns 85
cluster-shaped settlements 117
coastlines 6, 22, 24, 28–30, 36, 104–7
compass directions 51
conservation 6, 7, 8, 11, 124–5
contour maps 64–70
cross-sections 27, 66–8
cubic flow 27

dendritic drainage 96
dot distribution map 39, 72

employment 17, 113, 114, 115
energy 112, 114, 115
equipment and tools 23, 48
estimating area on a map 70–1

farming 7–8, 18–19, 24, 40–1, 112–13, 125, 126–7
field mapping 20, 35, 37
field notebooks 23, 25
field records 23–5
field sketching 35–6
field transect 20
flow diagram 19, 38

geology and scenery 86–9
glaciation 6, 37, 56–7, 64, 74, 108–11
gradients 69–70
graphs 76–81
grid references 52–3

heights on a map 65
histograms 80
hydro-electricity 101
hypothesis testing 12–13

igneous rocks 86, 90

impermeable rocks 86–7
industry 8, 38, 114–16, 124–5
inland waterways 103
inputs and outputs 7, 112–14
intermittent drainage 89, 96
interviews 44
isopleths 39, 72

land use 6, 7–8, 14, 19, 20–1, 24, 36, 40–1, 78, 81, 126–7
landforms on a map 93–4
leisure and recreation 11, 13, 109
limestones 88–9
line graph 77
line transect 20–1
linear scale 49–50
linear-shaped settlements 117
lines on a map 53
location of industries 8, 116
lowland river features 100

making comparisons 83–5
manufacturing processes 114
map interpretation 74–5
map measurements 50
map reading techniques 74–5
map scales 47–50
map scale 1:1 250 47
map scale 1:10 000 48
map scale 1:2 500 48
map scale 1:25 000 48, 55
map scale 1:50 000 48, 55
mean 81
measurements in the field 26–34
measuring amenities 33
measuring beach or river deposits 28–9
measuring erosion and deposition 29
measuring flow of a river 26–7
measuring longshore drift 30
mechanical weathering 91
median 81
metamorphic rocks 86
mode 81

National Grid 52
negative correlation 83–5
normal probability curve 80

Ordnance Survey map extract 1:25 000 58
Ordnance Survey map extract 1:50 000 56

patches on a map 53
patterns on a map 72–3
percentages 77, 82
permeable (pervious) rocks 86, 88–9
photographs 42–3, 57, 59, 60–3
pie chart 19, 78
planning an enquiry 14–15
points on a map 53
pollution 6, 8, 11, 42–3, 124–5

population 9, 77, 79, 81
positive correlation 83–5
printed source, use of 16–17, 76

quadrats 22
qualitative and quantitative observations 18–19
questionnaires 19, 44

random distribution 85
rank correlation 77, 83–5
record cards 23
representative fraction 49
river, uses of 102–3
rivers 5–7, 11, 20, 26–7, 37, 93, 96–103, 126–7
road transect 21
routeways 103

sample percentages 82
sampling methods 20–2, 82
scatter graphs 77, 83–5
sedimentary rocks 86–9
selective tracings 19, 72–3, 96
settlements 9–11, 117
shopping 4, 10, 44
sketch sections 68
slopes 69–70, 99
soil creep 92
soil erosion 92, 126–7
soil profile 92
soils 6–7, 90–2, 113
spot heights 64–5
statistics 17, 19, 76–85
symbols on a map 39, 53

tally counter 31
tally sheet 24
tape recordings 42
testing an idea 12–13
testing soils 91
town functions 121
town growth 118–19
town sites 120–1
traffic census 32
transects 20–2
transport and communications 8–9, 12, 102–3, 115, 116, 117, 124
trellised drainage 96
triangulation points 64–5

upland river features 97–8
urban hierarchies and hinterlands 122–3
urban topics 4, 8, 9–11, 12, 21–2, 33–4, 62–3, 117, 118–19, 120–1, 122–3, 124–5
urban transects 21–2

water cycle 95
water supply 6, 102, 124
watershed 96
weathering 90–1